LEGENDS ON TOUR

The Pop Package Tours
of the 1960s

The excitement builds in the audience. (*Aldershot News*)

Martin Creasy

LEGENDS ON TOUR

The Pop Package Tours of the 1960s

TEMPUS

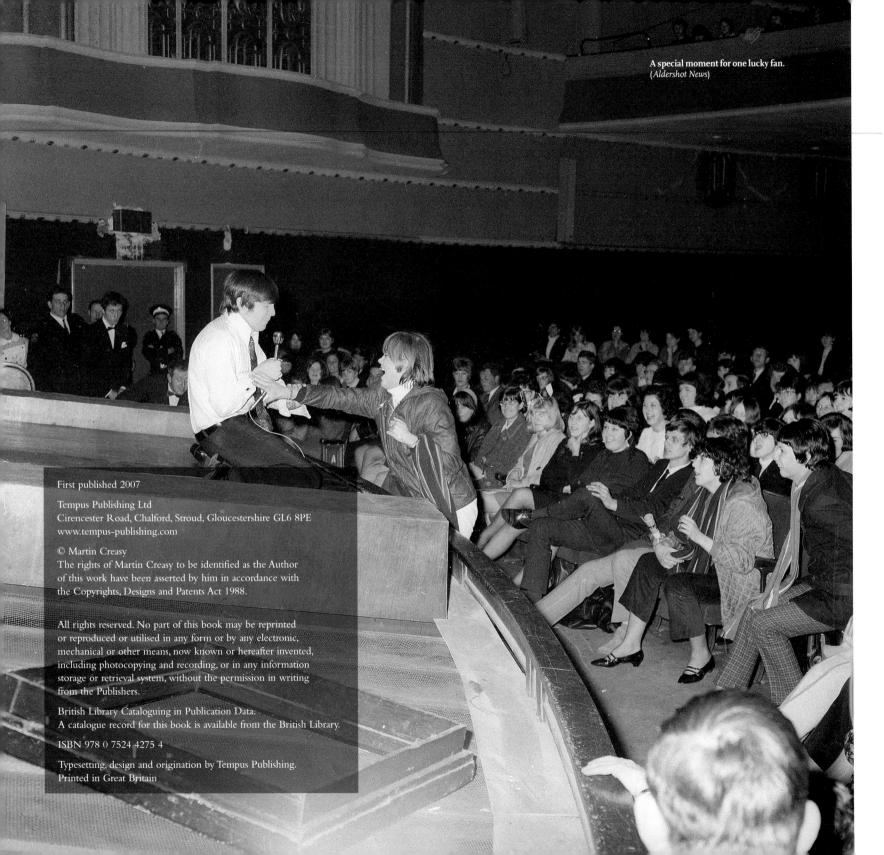

A special moment for one lucky fan.
(*Aldershot News*)

First published 2007

Tempus Publishing Ltd
Cirencester Road, Chalford, Stroud, Gloucestershire GL6 8PE
www.tempus-publishing.com

© Martin Creasy
The rights of Martin Creasy to be identified as the Author
of this work have been asserted by him in accordance with
the Copyrights, Designs and Patents Act 1988.

British Library Cataloguing in Publication Data.
A catalogue record for this book is available from the British Library.

ISBN 978 0 7524 4275 4

Typesetting, design and origination by Tempus Publishing.
Printed in Great Britain

Running Order

Author's Note

WOULDN'T IT BE great if you could press a button and just for a short while be transported back in time to relive something wonderful from your past, or even catch up on something you missed out on?

Technology has come a long way, but it has not quite managed that yet. Pop fans did not have top quality DVD players in the early 1960s, nor did they have iPods or computers to download the latest sounds from their favourite stars. Vinyl was precious as fans waited eagerly for the new record in single, EP or LP form, but what those 1960s teens did have was the joy of being able to see the biggest pop stars in the world performing, sometimes en masse, in their local High Street, perhaps at the cinema or maybe the town hall.

This book looks in detail at seven of these pop package tours that reached the Aldershot ABC Cinema, one of the regular venues. We will follow the trail across the country with anecdotes from stars and fans and many previously unseen pictures to bring those stories to life.

No 1960s pop book could be complete without a section on the Beatles and so we will start by looking at the Fab Four's exploits on the road, plus the memories of Helen Shapiro who had the honour of topping the bill on the Beatles' first UK pop package tour. This took place at the beginning of 1963 when Britain was shivering in the grip of its worst winter in years, so don't forget your coat...

Thanks

THIS BOOK COULD not have happened without the support, generosity and kindness of a number of people who it would be very remiss of me not to thank.

I would like to start with the *Aldershot News* for permission to use the photographs and in particular their four photographers responsible for the wonderful concert pictures from Aldershot, namely Brian Bramley, Eddie Trusler, Mike Hawley and Jeff Trolley. Their skill in capturing the emotion, excitement and drama is there for all to behold. Many newspapers, when they moved offices, had to reluctantly dispose of their pictures from the 1960s and 1970s, but Brian was responsible for saving up to 80,000 negatives and pictures which are now safely housed at Aldershot's Military Museum.

An enormous thank you is also due the *Leicester Mercury* for their generous contribution of Beatle concert pictures and in particular staff member Neil Evans.

Thanks also go to the *East Anglian Daily Times* and the *Bournemouth Daily Echo* and respective staffers Sharon Boswell and Scott Harrison, and also to Howard Portman, son of the renowned Bournemouth photographer Harry Portman. Wolverhampton and Bournemouth libraries and their respective staff members, Alf Russell and Jan Marsh, are also thanked.

The author is grateful to every one of the fans and 1960s pop stars interviewed. Each one gave generously of their time, energy and memories.

Particular thanks to Aldershot librarian Stephen Phillips, whose help and support I came to rely on.

Thanks also to Beatles authors Mark Lewisohn and Barry Miles whose remarkable books made the perfect reference point for cross checking my facts, and also to Terry Rawlings, author of *British Beat 1960–1969*.

The *NME* and *Disc* were vital for referencing dates and set lists and so my thanks go to them also.

Thanks to Tempus for having faith in the project and to Amy Rigg who always answered my countless calls and questions with remarkable patience.

And a big bouquet to my dear Pravina for putting up with me having my head buried in all this for so much of the past three years.

Reg Presley of the Troggs discovers that love really is all around. (*Aldershot News*)

One
The Fabulous Beatles

Roll up, roll up for the magical Beatles tours

THE GAUMONT CINEMA in Bradford had the distinction of hosting the first Beatles performance as part of a pop package tour. The date was Saturday 2 February 1963 and on the coach with the Fab Four were teenage sensation Helen Shapiro, who was topping the bill, singers Danny Williams and Kenny Lynch, plus the Red Price Band, the Honeys, and the Kestrels. The compère was Dave Allen.

This was a period of great excitement for the Beatles. Their second single, *Please Please Me*, released on Friday 11 January, reached the coveted number one spot in the *NME* chart on 19 February. The Beatles were told the great news just before they went on stage at the Cavern during a small break in the tour. By the time the tour resumed at the Granada Cinema, Mansfield, on 23 February, the Beatles were also top of the chart listed by *Disc*.

The national press was still some months away from discovering their magic and the Beatles were not bill-toppers yet, but it was obvious from the reception they were starting to get up and down the country that they were destined for stardom.

Following that opening night the tour rocked on to the Gaumont Cinema in Doncaster on the Tuesday, the Granada in Bedford the next night and the Regal Cinema in Wakefield on Thursday 7 February.

It seems hard to believe that the Beatles were effectively bottom of the bill at the start of the tour, performing four songs in the first half. However, they were soon to be closing before the interval, effectively making them the main supporting act. They sang *Chains, Keep Your Hands Off My Baby, A Taste Of Honey* and *Please Please Me*. Two other numbers, *Beautiful Dreamer* and their debut single, *Love Me Do*, were substitute songs for the tour.

The street is packed with fans queuing for tickets for the Beatles' show at the De Montfort Hall, Leicester. It all looks peaceful enough, but note that the policeman has his dog at the ready... (Courtesy of the *Leicester Mercury*)

On stage, the Beatles were dressed in smart burgundy suits with velvet collars, with John and Paul developing a new tactic of rushing to the mike together and shaking their heads and singing shrill falsetto 'oohs' to make the girls scream louder. Off stage, however, they preferred to resort to their leather jackets and it brought them some unfavourable attention at a town centre hotel following the tour's fifth date at the ABC Cinema in Warwick Road, Carlisle, on Friday 8 February. The boys, along with Helen and Kenny, suffered the embarrassment of being asked to leave a dance at the posh Crown and Mitre Hotel, reportedly because the leather Beatle look was deemed too tacky for the up-market ballroom. The story was blown up into a major incident by a national newspaper and so it was red faces under the mop tops at the Empire Theatre on High Street, Sunderland, the next night as the Beatles made their last appearance before the tour took its short break.

For most stars the coach tours were gruelling enough on their own. The Beatles' schedule would have sent lesser people running for cover. The small break in this tour represented no break for them. Instead they headed down to the Abbey Road studios in London on Monday 11 February, to record ten tracks to complete their debut LP, *Please Please Me*. The album mainly consisted of favourites from their Cavern gig list and they completed the job, unbelievably, in that single day. Just as unbelievably, the final track was John's throat-tearing *Twist and Shout*.

The next five nights were taken up with concerts that manager Brian Epstein had long-since booked and then it was back to London to mime *Please Please Me* for the *Thank Your Lucky Stars* television show on Sunday 17 February.

Next night it was Widnes and then it was the Cavern. Following the Cavern performance, they drove through the night down to London to sing *Love Me Do* and *Please Please Me* for BBC radio's *Parade of the Pops* on Wednesday 20 February. From there they set off on a daunting 160-mile trek to Doncaster for that night's live performance.

Gigs followed at Birkenhead and Manchester on the next two nights before the tour resumed at Mansfield on Saturday 23 February. It reached the Coventry Theatre the next night, followed swiftly by trips to the Gaumont Cinema at Taunton and the Rialto Theatre at York. The harsh winter took its toll on Helen, who succumbed to a cold and missed the Taunton and York dates. Billie Davis, who was in the charts with *Tell Him*, was drafted in for those two shows. South African star Danny Williams, of *Moon River* fame, took over as bill topper until Helen returned to play the Granada Cinema, Shrewsbury, on Thursday 28 February.

The Beatles penned their next single, *From Me To You*, while on the tour bus heading from York to Shrewsbury. The renowned songwriter Roger Greenaway, then a humble member of the Kestrels, later recalled during a lighthearted BBC radio interview how Kenny Lynch had joined John and Paul at the back of the coach while they were working on the song. What a load of rubbish, Kenny laughed, as they strummed away. I wonder if he was still smiling when the song hit number one a few weeks later? Never mind, Kenny had the honour of being the first non-Beatle to record a Beatles song. They had just finished writing *Misery* with the intention of offering it to Helen; however, Norrie Paramor, Helen's A&R man, rejected the offer without Helen's knowledge and Kenny recorded it instead.

There were three dates left: the Odeon at Southport on Friday 1 March, the City Hall, Sheffield, the next night, and the Gaumont Cinema in Hanley, Staffordshire, on Sunday 3 March.

(Left) **Smiles all round as the Beatles greet children before their performance at the Ipswich Gaumont on Wednesday 22 May 1963, on their tour with Roy Orbison and Gerry and the Pacemakers. (***East Anglian Daily Times***)**

(Right) **'Baby you can drive my car...' Perhaps this is where George's love of motor racing began as the Beatles relaxed before their show at the Winter Gardens, Bournemouth, on Saturday 16 November 1963. (***Bournemouth Daily Echo***)**

Superstars in the making, the Beatles surely were. However, they suffered the same restrictions as all the other performers in those down to earth days. When they got back to their digs after performances, the adrenalin still pumping from all the excitement, they liked to unwind with their favourite scotch and coke and swap stories with the other performers until they were finally ready to crash. Unfortunately, they were not yet staying in five-star luxury and sometimes the bar was shut. Ringo later told of having to beg for a sandwich made hours earlier from the long-closed dining room when they returned to their small hotel, tired and hungry after their night's work. The usual answer was 'no'.

Nevertheless, the humble three- and four-star hotels were palaces compared to what the Beatles were used to. Deep carpets and uniformed waiters appeared the height of luxury for Beatles who had not long since bedded down in a grimy room in Hamburg's infamous Reeperbahn district.

Late nights on tour would be followed by late mornings, and then it was all aboard the coach for the long haul to the next venue. It was an annoyance that they sometimes had to travel long distances, only to return for a gig the next night just a few miles from the venue they had already played.

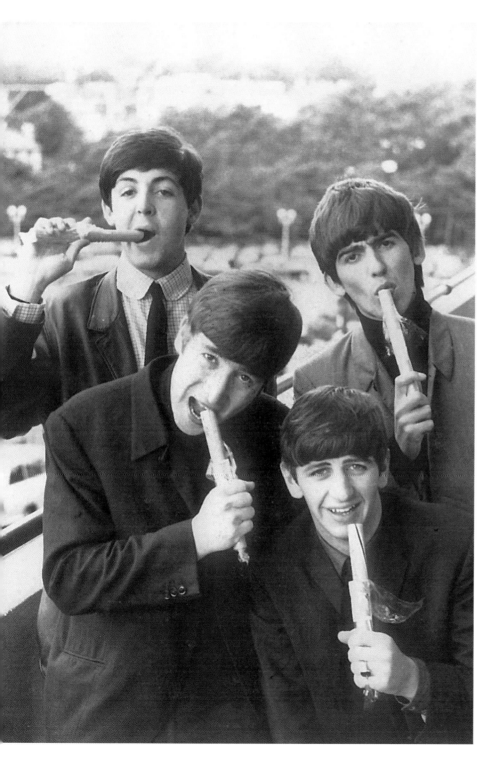

'Oh we do like to be beside the seaside...' The Beatles show they are a rock group on the balcony of the Palace Court Hotel in Bournemouth. (*Bournemouth Daily Echo*, copyright Harry/Howard Portman)

Beatles road manager Neil Aspinall recalled how unprepared he was for dealing with the light and sound systems at theatres and cinemas equally unprepared for staging rock and roll shows. Cinema staff who took over lighting and sound duties at picture houses were little better, sometimes training the spotlight on Paul when John was singing and vice versa. Soundchecks consisted of the Beatles running through numbers on stage, while Neil stationed himself at various points in the auditorium. The results were usually very disappointing. Beatle amplifiers were reliable enough, but house systems in theatres, cinemas and small concert halls were not up to the job. Even the mikes were only of sufficient quality to talk through.

Helen Shapiro, as the star turn, had been offered a car for the tour by promoter Arthur Howes. She rarely used it because she was enjoying the camaraderie of the tour bus – particularly enjoying the company of her cheeky new Beatle friends. She told the *Beatles Book* fan magazine of how they strummed away at the back of the coach, sometimes working hard on their harmonies or new songs, and at other moments raucously singing some rude ditty. Sometimes they would play cards, particularly George and Ringo if John and Paul were embroiled in the complexities of working out another new song.

Helen's verdict on each Beatle was pretty much typical – Paul was charming and excellent for the group's PR, while George was sincere, intelligent and keen to learn everything about the music business. Helen enjoyed many long conversations with Ringo and his dry wit would often prompt a burst of the giggles. John was already developing a reputation of being the most dangerous Beatle to deal with. He could be aggressive and cutting and did not suffer fools. However, in Helen's case he was protective and charming. Helen's verdict was that he would make a good husband and father one day. She did not know, of course, that John was already married and that his wife, Cynthia, was to give birth to a bouncing boy on Monday 8 April, little more than a month after the end of the tour!

Luckily, the boys had plenty of energy. It was a mere five days before they commenced another pop package tour, in between fitting in an EMI recording session, the taping of a radio show and three stage performances.

This second package tour began on Saturday 9 March, at the Gaumont in East Ham, London. Joint bill toppers this time were Americans Chris Montez and Tommy Roe, but their moment in the spotlight on this tour was to be limited.

Montez made the mistake of generously allowing the Beatles to take top spot when the tour played the Liverpool Empire on Sunday 24 March. The reaction to the Fabs in their home city persuaded tour bosses that the mop-tops should be the show-closers from now on. Completing the tour line-up were the Viscounts, Debbie Lee and the Terry Young Six. Tony Marsh was the compère.

The Beatles sang six tracks from their debut LP, *Love Me Do*, *Misery*, *A Taste Of Honey*, *Do You Want To Know A Secret*, *Please Please Me* and a rousing finish with *I Saw Her Standing There*.

The only nights off until the tour finished at the De Montfort Hall, Leicester, on Sunday 31 March, were Monday 11 March when the Beatles spent the evening holed-up at EMI House in London recording chat for a show on Radio Luxembourg and Monday

25 March when photographer Dezo Hoffmann grabbed them for a photo session.

John was a brief casualty of that elongated winter. He went down with a heavy cold and missed the shows at the Granada cinema in Bedford on Tuesday 12 March, the Rialto Theatre, York, and the Gaumont Cinema in Wolverhampton, before returning at the Colston Hall, Bristol, on Friday 15 March. Those performances without John would have been unique. George and Paul coped with John's vocal lines on *Please Please Me* to very good effect, according to a newspaper report on the Rialto performance, and Paul threw in *Till There Was You* to make up the numbers.

John's absence did not merit a comment in a brief report in the *Wolverhampton Express and Star*, which simply said of their efforts, 'The Beatles, with their unusual haircuts, did well to emerge from a particularly ill-mannered audience buffeting with credit.'

They would have to get used to such ill manners. On and on rolled the show into Sheffield, Peterborough, Gloucester, Cambridge, Romford, Croydon, Doncaster and Newcastle, before reaching the boys' home town on Sunday 24 March, for those two houses at the Liverpool Empire.

There were just six more towns after this: Mansfield, Northampton, Exeter, Lewisham, Portsmouth, and the farewell night at the De Montfort Hall in Leicester.

Their hectic schedule continued right up to their third package tour which started at the Adelphi in Slough on Saturday 18 May, with Roy Orbison as the star of the show. However, organisers were soon ordering reprints of the tour programme, with the Beatles this time appearing first, in glorious red lettering! Also on the bill were their old mates Gerry and the Pacemakers, plus the Terry Young Six, Geordie crooner David Macbeth, singers Louise Cordet and Ian Crawford, plus Erkey Grant. The compère was Tony Marsh.

The boys added Cavern favourite *Some Other Guy* to a gig list that featured six other songs – *Do You Want To Know A Secret*, *Love Me Do*, *From Me To You*, *Please Please Me*, *I Saw Her Standing There* and *Twist And Shout*.

For just over three weeks the tour wended its way up and down the country, with only two nights off. On one of those – Tuesday 21 May – they were kept busy with a solid day's radio work, but Thursday 6 June was a rare luxury indeed – a real day off!

Roy Orbison was a slick performer, and the boys were slightly in awe of him, even though the spotlight was increasingly on them. Night after night it was the Beatles who were greeted with screams.

Orbison also brought out their competitive edge that was a crucial factor in the success of the Fab Four. Roy, at the back of the coach, would casually strum a new song he was putting together and Beatle ears would quickly pick up the vibes of a craftsman at work. Their unspoken response was to come up with something even better.

Touring meant John and Paul were spending virtually every waking moment in each other's company and for a comparatively brief period

One girl who got too carried away at the De Montfort Hall, Leicester, gets carried away by security. Note the girls standing hotfoot on the radiators craning for a view of the Beatles. (Courtesy of the *Leicester Mercury*)

Lennon and McCartney songs were just that, joint efforts, both making major contributions to each song and both sharing major vocal lines.

Pretty soon it would be simple for fans to work out which were McCartney's efforts and which were Lennon's – the rough guide being the one who sang lead wrote the song. But for now John and Paul were as one, their competitive spirit focused on sweeping aside all comers, rather than flexing their muscles for superiority within the group.

Shows in intimate theatres and cinemas meant fans got close enough to smother the Beatles, and Aspinall soon had to learn yet another skill – how to sneak them in and out of venues without being mobbed.

A really lucky fan might even get to spend some time with them, perhaps accompanying a local journalist on a complimentary pass, as Irene Snidall did when the tour reached Sheffield City Hall on Saturday 25 May. All four signed her precious copy of their debut album that night and she witnessed the Beatles' dressing room banter at first hand. It was a full year before the rest of the world could enjoy that banter when *A Hard Day's Night* packed cinemas up and down the country.

Radio was as powerful as television in the early 1960s and the Beatles had already made a huge impact over the airwaves. It was a

sign of their increasing power that they secured their very own radio show – *Pop Go The Beatles* – which aired for the first time on Tuesday 4 June, when the tour was winding its way into Birmingham ready to take the town hall by storm.

A few days later, on Friday 7 June, the tour popped over the border to Scotland for a show at the Odeon Cinema in Glasgow. The city had a reputation as a graveyard for performers who were not up to scratch. There was no such problem for the Beatles. They played several more Glasgow dates during their career and loved the reception they got from their Scottish fans.

The tour wound up with a finale at King George's Hall in Blackburn two nights later. There were plenty more gigs packed in that summer, plus a growing round of radio and television dates to keep the Beatles busy. They then returned to London on Monday 1 July to record *She Loves You*, their biggest hit so far and a song that was to launch them into a new stratosphere.

They enjoyed a holiday at the end of September, before returning to their hectic new life. 13 October was another milestone: they starred at the Sunday Night at the London Palladium, introduced by compère Bruce Forsyth, and the British media finally got the message. Beatlemania was born.

On Monday 4 November, they were seventh on a bill of nineteen acts at the Royal Command Performance in front of the Queen Mother and Princess Margaret. It was screened the following Sunday and confirmed their status as the number one act in Britain. Soon it was to be the world.

A few days before that historic performance, the Beatles began a daunting autumn UK tour that started out at the Odeon Cinema in Cheltenham on Friday 1 November and took in thirty-four dates, finishing at the Gaumont Cinema in Southampton on Friday 13 December. Joining the Beatles on this tour were the Rhythm & Blues Quartet, the Vernons Girls, the Brook Brothers, Peter Jay and the Jaywalkers, and the Kestrels. The compère was Frank Berry. This time, at long last, the Beatles were officially top of the bill from the start. They had time for a few more songs, not that the fans, or the Beatles themselves, could hear much over the din.

Their ten-number gig list remained constant throughout the tour, taking in several songs from their second album, *With The Beatles*, which was released in the middle of the tour on the fateful day of 22 November when John F. Kennedy was assassinated in Dallas. They kicked off each night with *I Saw Her Standing There*, followed by *From Me To You, All My Loving, You Really Got A Hold On Me, Roll Over Beethoven, Boys, Till There Was You, She Loves You* and *Money* before John hit them with the show-closer, *Twist And Shout*.

By this time the tour bus had become impractical, so it was the good old group van, or perhaps a car to ferry the boys around. They had a new Ford Zephyr which Neil Aspinall would drive them around in, although they sometimes used a decoy car to try to find some respite from invading fans who could now be numbered in their thousands.

The magazine also published a picture of Paul doodling on the piano with Tony Burrows of the Kestrels that night. The accompanying article recorded how the boys had time for a quick wash between the two 'houses' and how Neil Aspinall, apart from all his other duties, would see that the Beatle diet of steak and chips, washed down with Pepsi or tea, was maintained.

The Beatles made much bigger headlines, this time in the *Wolverhampton Express and Star*. The paper recounted a tale of mass hysteria at the Gaumont, with teens rushing the stage during the Beatles set, bottles and jelly babies being thrown and hundreds of girls weeping uncontrollably at the end. A ticketless girl staged a feigned suicide attempt when turned away, the paper reporting that at least some of the tablets she swallowed were peppermints.

The hysteria continued outside with thousands of screaming youngsters gathering under the dressing room window for the chance of a glimpse of the Beatles. They were kept off the road by crash barriers and the police.

About two dozen youngsters gathered outside the local hospital where roadie Mal Evans was recovering after crashing the group's van the previous day. The teenagers suspected the group would visit him, but their schedule proved too tight. The concert mayhem was captured in a photograph under the heading Beatlemania!

With all the mayhem, little could be heard of the Beatles music and it was proving to be the same wherever they went. Their humour was holding up, however. A Beatle reply to one question went, 'Yes, we are doing a film set in Korea. It has to be there because we are Koreans. There, John has his leg amputated.'

Their new single *I Want To Hold Your Hand* was released on Friday 29 November as the tour was headed for that night's gig at the ABC Cinema in Huddersfield. There were advanced sales of more than a million – the first time this had happened in pop history.

In between the two shows that night an up-and-coming young man from the Huddersfield Tape Recording Society conducted separate interviews with each Beatle for a hospital radio programme. The young man – Gordon Kaye – would some years later be giving interviews of his own after he captured hearts as René in the BBC sitcom *'Allo 'Allo*.

The show at the De Montfort Hall, Leicester, on Sunday 1 December was typically chaotic, with several hundred police on virtual riot patrol and shocked stewards and St John Ambulance crew under siege. A boy leapt off a balcony straight onto the stage and threw his arms around the neck of a startled Beatle at the finale of the second house.

Steward Ray Millward, aged fifty-nine, was counting his bruises. He told the *Leicester Mercury*:

I have never seen anything like this. We used to get a lot of hysteria with Cliff Richard, but this beats everything. I had a shoe and umbrella thrown at me. One girl fought like a wildcat. I had to force her arm behind her back to get her to sit down. She was scratching, kicking and screaming the whole time.

There were tears on the South Coast on Tuesday 12 November, when the gig at the Portsmouth Guildhall was postponed after Paul was hit with a bout of gastric flu. The Beatles were never ones to let their fans down, however, and they went back to play the gig on Tuesday 3 December on what would have been a night off.

A front page of the *Bournemouth Evening Echo* the previous month had provided evidence of how valuable tickets were. A photograph showed three teenage girls huddled in a blanket camping outside the Winter Gardens for more than two days to be sure of their tickets for the show on Saturday 16 November. The girls held up copies of music papers to cover their faces, claiming their parents and bosses did not know they were there. It was worth it, however, when they got prime tickets to see the Fab Four. Not everyone did, though. The theatre returned a cheque for £134 10s for 316 tickets to the Junior Leaders Regiment at Bovington Camp!

The screaming was relentless by now. The Beatles' two 20-minute spots that night were almost inaudible and there was pandemonium getting in and out of the Winter Gardens. Despite the mayhem, the Beatles still managed to find some normality. The *Beatles Book* magazine editor Johnny Dean visited the boys when the show reached the Gaumont Cinema in Wolverhampton on Tuesday 19 November. He took some pictures of the Beatles on stage before the shows. They were in their stage suits and playing, as if to an audience. He witnessed a 15-minute jam session featuring John Lennon, plus Peter Jay and 'Lolly' Lloyd Baker of the Jaywalkers and the lead guitarist of the Rhythm & Blues Quartet.

(*Above*) 1 December 1963, and the kids go wild for the Beatles at the De Montfort Hall in Leicester. (Courtesy of the *Leicester Mercury*)

(*Left*) The girls at the De Montford Hall, Leicester, go mad for the Beatles. (Courtesy of the *Leicester Mercury*)

Fan Barbara Corderoy is the hands-down winner of the most amusing comment award when she told the newspaper:

'I didn't hear anything … I didn't see anything … but it was Fab!'

The Beatles at the De Montfort Hall, Leicester, in December 1963. (Courtesy of the *Leicester Mercury*)

The night after the tour finished at Southampton, the Beatles played a gig at Wimbledon for their southern fan club. The following week the Beatles' Christmas Show began a sixteen-night run at the Astoria in Finsbury Park.

Europe and the world beckoned in 1964, but the truth is there had been a big change in the Beatles during the tumultuous year of 1963. The optimism and excitement of the early months had disappeared by the end of the year. They were savvy enough to protect their ever-smiling happy-go-lucky mop-top image. But underneath the haircuts, the Beatles were resentful that they had gone backwards as a live act as they played gig after gig to the constant accompaniment of screams that made them inaudible. Doubling the size of their amps had made no difference.

America was still to be conquered and the Beatles were happy to leave cold, damp Britain behind for a while as they set off in search of a new challenge.

It was ten months before they would embark on another huge tour of the UK. When they did it was with some reluctance – an answer to the jibe that they had forgotten their fans back home.

Memories came flooding back of being imprisoned in cramped dressing rooms in run-down cinemas and theatres. The enormous stadiums of America had caused problems of their own as Beatlemania grew, but now this definitely seemed like a step backwards as they faced the grim march of another autumn tour of the UK.

This kicked off at the Gaumont Cinema, Bradford, on Friday 9 October 1964. Mary Wells was a special guest on the tour, which also featured fellow Liverpudlian Tommy Quickly, backed by the Remo Four, plus Sounds Incorporated, the Rustiks and Michael Haslam. Bob Bain was the compère. The tour was the usual format of two houses a night, starting at 6.15 p.m. and 8.40 p.m. It meant fifty-four shows at twenty-seven venues in little over a month. Fans paid a top price of 10s 6d, down to 5s 6d in the cheap seats.

Mary had won her spot on the bill not least because the Fab Four loved her song *My Guy* which had been a big hit that summer. They were also happy for her to conduct the press interviews as they were bored with them.

Anyone around the Bradford cinema on that opening afternoon may have heard a nice bonus – four Beatles playing a song they were part-way through recording. *I Feel Fine* was to hit the shops six weeks later and they worked on it on the stage that Friday afternoon with all doors and entrances firmly locked!

The Beatles were paid £850 a night on this tour, so at least there was some compensation for what had long since become a chore.

The opening night produced fantastic scenes, with banner-waving fans trying to break through police barriers and all sorts of objects being lobbed towards the stage, including a giant teddy for John, who was celebrating his twenty-fourth birthday.

The Beatles, in smart, black suits, opened with a short burst of *Twist And Shout* and then launched straight into *Money*. A short thank you speech by Paul preceded *Can't Buy Me Love*, followed by four more tracks from the *A Hard Day's Night* LP, *Things We Said Today*, *I'm Happy Just To Dance With You*, *I Should Have Known Better* and *If I Fell*. Ringo pitched in with *I Wanna Be Your Man*. John then led the way for *A Hard Day's Night* and then Paul took over for the show-closer, the Little Richard rocker *Long Tall Sally*. These were their ten songs for the tour.

Even an artist as talented as Mary Wells struggled with an audience there totally to see the Fab Four. She had closed the first half, wearing a pink dress for the first house and a black for the second, but the reception was the same – lukewarm. Her big song *My Guy* went down well, but *What's So Easy For Two Is So Hard For One*, *Time After Time* and *Two Lovers* went over quite a few teeny heads.

Mary was backed by Sounds Incorporated and they tried hard in their own slot, with *Spanish Harlem* followed by *Maria* from West Side Story. Tommy Quickly had the slot before the Beatles and he fared a bit better. He looked quite a sight decked out in a bowler hat, with an umbrella in one hand and a toy dog in the other for *Walkin' The Dog*. The knockabout theme continued with *Humpty Dumpty* and he got his biggest cheer for his single, and the nearest he ever came to a hit, *The Wild Side Of Life*.

The old decoy car routine had long since been rumbled by the fans and the Beatles' getaway from the De Montfort Hall, Leicester, the next night was chaotic, despite the best laid plans. The great idea was that the boys would be bundled into a black saloon at the back while the National Anthem was still playing. Unfortunately, the teens were not respectfully standing and saluting Her Majesty. A mob of sixty to seventy girls rumbled the ruse and swarmed around the Beatlemobile in University Road, hammering on the windows and roof. The saloon careered into another car in the panic before the police finally managed to free them.

On stage it had been the same old story: the Beatles played on despite mass fainting and screaming. *Mercury* reporter Denis Downes – fingers in ears – had taken his twelve-year-old daughter to the show and he captured the chaos in his amusing column:

A shower of jelly babies rained round the unfortunate men on the stage, ricocheting off the impassive line of policemen, stewards and ambulancemen looking stolidly outwards from the front of the hall.

John (or was it George?) ducked nimbly and a half pound block of chocolate, suitably wrapped, hurtled past his left ear.

A special day for Helen Shapiro, as she waltzes with John Lennon during a break in filming for *Ready Steady Go.* (David Redfern, Redfern Music Picture Library)

And so the mayhem went on up and down the country. There were dates again in Scotland and even a gig at the King's Hall in Belfast before the finale at the Colston Hall, Bristol, on Tuesday 10 November.

As we will come to discover, last night equalled prank night on many tours. It normally involved the artists playing tricks on each other, but at the Colston Hall it was a naughty group of students who left the Beatles, if not with egg on their faces, with a considerable amount of flour in their hair. The Fab Four were singing *If I Fell* when the not-so-fab four students, who were perched up in the stage lighting gantries, tipped bags of flour on them. Hall manager Ken Cowley was reportedly not amused by the breach of security, but the Beatles simply shook their heads in that Beatle style, grinned and carried on.

The group was to embark on only one more UK tour – more than a year later – and there was even more reluctance. After protracted talks between Epstein and promoter Arthur Howes, they agreed to play just nine dates.

With them this time were the Moody Blues, plus the Paramounts, the nucleus of whom went on to become Procol Harum, and some scouse mates – singers Beryl Marsden and Steve Aldo and a group called the Koobas.

The Beatles had outgrown their teenybop image. The opening date at the Odeon in Glasgow on Friday 3 December 1965 coincided with the release of their new album *Rubber Soul* and their music was developing rapidly.

Their tour numbers were *I Feel Fine, She's A Woman, If I Needed Someone, Act Naturally, Nowhere Man, Baby's In Black, Help! We Can Work It Out, Yesterday, Day Tripper* and *I'm Down*. The tour included a farewell to Liverpool – two sell-out houses of 2,500 at the Empire with Paul even joining the Koobas on drums for the Larry Williams rocker *Dizzy Miss Lizzy*.

This final British tour ended at the Capitol Cinema, Cardiff, on Sunday 12 December, and by the end of the following summer the group had turned their back on touring for good.

...and on your next tour, Helen, is this new band, the Beatles

More than forty years may have passed, but Helen Shapiro still has vivid – and fond – memories of that early 1963 pop package tour with the Beatles:

The first time I met them was at what we called a band call – a rehearsal, basically. The Beatles were already on stage, setting up, when I was introduced to them. It was Paul who was their spokesman. He was very bright and chirpy and he introduced me to the others. I remember them being very upbeat and excited. After all, this was a national tour and they hadn't done one of those before. They had played the Cavern, Hamburg and the ballrooms, all that stuff, but this was quite different.

The Beatles had only enjoyed one minor hit at this stage. Their debut disc, *Love Me Do*, released in October 1962, had only scraped into the top twenty, but Helen, at sixteen and a good four or five years younger than them, was already a fan.

I'd had a meeting with Arthur Howes and he'd said that for this new tour I'd be accompanied by Danny Williams and Kenny Lynch and that the Red Price combo would be my backing band. Dave Allen would be the compère and there would also be this new group called the Beatles.

He asked if I'd heard of them and of course, I had. I loved their song *Love Me Do* and I was looking forward to the tour. Dave Allen didn't have a halfpenny to his name in those days, but he was a lovely guy and very funny. I was always touring with Danny and Kenny, and so I knew them well. The great songwriter Roger Greenaway was a member of the Kestrels, who were also on this tour.

Howes was later to become Helen's agent. 'He put on nearly all of those tours and he was a big guy in the business, very brave and innovative. In fact, it was Arthur who first took a chance on bringing over all those Tamla stars, Marvin Gaye, Mary Wells, Little Stevie Wonder and the rest.'

Helen said John and Paul had written *Misery* before the tour started and she only discovered that Norrie Paramor had rejected it when she chatted to Paul. 'It was a done deal. I knew nothing about it. I was a bit upset that nobody had told me. Of course, the Beatles hadn't made their name as songwriters yet, but I was disappointed. Then again, I was still a kid. I was only sixteen.'

Helen, or Helly as she was affectionately known by the Fab Four, recalled the coach singalongs:

We were all on the coach and we all used to sing together. The Beatles would be strumming away and sometimes I would take the lead, with them harmonising, and sometimes other people would be singing. They used to sing all sorts, but I remember them doing Beach Boys songs – they liked the Beach Boys back then. They also introduced us to all that Tamla Motown stuff that they loved. None of us had heard it before but I guess Brian Epstein had first dibs on it all because he had run the record shop (Nems). I would probably be singing Little Eva songs too, stuff like that.

John would sometimes be pulling faces at people out of the window. That was so typical of him. I had a big crush on John. I was mad about him.

Before one gig Paul and John asked a special favour of Helen. They wanted her opinion on two new songs they had written. Would *From Me To You* or *Thank You Girl* make the best A-side for their next single?

'There was a piano at the side of the stage and Paul sat down and played and John was standing at the side and they sang the songs. I told them that I thought *From Me To You* was better and they said we kind of thought that but wanted confirmation.'

At the start of the tour, the Honeys opened the show and the Beatles followed them for their four numbers. Things were soon to change.

It sort of gradually built up really. After *Please Please Me* hit the charts, that's what started things. It wasn't out of hand yet – Beatlemania

stand at the side of the stage and watch the Beatles' performance, and of course I had a crush on John.'

The night they were asked to leave the dance at the Crown and Mitre Hotel after the Carlisle gig is still etched on the memory:

It was the *Daily Express* that ran the story. I remember the headline was something like Helen Shapiro Asked To Leave Golf Club Dance, something like that. It referred to Helen Shapiro and 'The instrumental group the Four Beatles' being asked to leave. I was mortified. I thought that would be the end of me. It was terrible. I was only sixteen and that sort of thing was not something to be proud of then. I never found out for certain who tipped off the press.

Helen said the incident genuinely was something out of nothing:

We'd got back to the hotel and we were in the lobby area. Kenny and the Beatles were having a drink and I think I was having a cup of tea. This fellow was going into the banqueting suite when he saw us. He was really chuffed and asked us to go in. We weren't interested. They were all dressed up and it wasn't our kind of thing. We were just having a quiet drink, but he was really insistent. They had food in there – a buffet – and that probably swung it. We never seemed to get much to eat on tour.

We went to the buffet table and had something to eat. Ringo was particularly enjoying the food. Then we went on to the floor to dance – we may have still been eating. I think I was twisting with Ringo. There were these ladies with their long gowns who made a beeline for the Beatles in their leather gear.

Then suddenly this guy came over, a much older man, and he was huffing and puffing, getting red in the face. He ordered us to leave. Who invited you, he asked? The paper made a big fuss about it, but that was all there was to it.

It was a shame really because nobody seemed to have a problem with us, apart from the one bloke. The others accepted us.

hadn't started – but there was screaming for the Beatles. But they weren't screaming over them, during the songs. They would finish a number and that's when they screamed.

I was still pulling in my fans, and they were pulling in theirs. They were moved up to close the first half, probably about halfway through the tour.

The fans always saw it as a bit of a challenge to track down where the stars were staying.

We were in this hotel in Sheffield and the kids found out where we were. They were outside screaming and shouting for the Beatles and me, and we were throwing photos from a hotel lounge window.

I remember George used to practise signing his autograph – on cigarette packets, anything he could find, even other people's pictures. I just loved everything about those coach tours back then. Of course, the novelty wore off a bit later on when I realised what blooming hard work they were!

Helen was keen to correct one myth: 'Somebody wrote that the Beatles were often in my dressing room because I was the only one with a telly. What a laugh. None of the places we played had a telly. I used to

Paul makes time for an ice cream as the Beatles get ready to rock the Ipswich Gaumont to its rafters in 1964. (East Anglian Daily Times)

Despite her tender years, Helen was a veteran of the pop package tour by then, having been in the business two years, and with the hit records to match.

They were given a good airing on this tour, including her latest single, *Queen For Tonight*. It hit the charts on 7 February as the tour headed for that night's gig at the Regal Cinema in Wakefield. The Carlisle hiccup happened the next night.

Among the other hits Helen belted out in her 25-minute set would have been *Don't Treat Me Like A Child*, *You Don't Know*, *Tell Me What He Said* and the blockbuster *Walkin' Back To Happiness*. 'I would probably have thrown in a slow bluesy type number as well, as I was into jazz and blues,' said Helen.

Helen recalls that the coach was warm enough, despite the snow and bitter cold of that winter, but it did have one discomfort. 'It was very smoky, I remember that. I couldn't complain, though, because I was adding to it. I was a secret smoker at that stage, though I have long since given up.'

Despite all the success, and the title of one of her hits, Helen was still a child and had to endure a chaperon on tour. 'It was probably the law. My parents were proud of my success, but, of course, they were concerned for me. I would occasionally take them to gigs. They missed me and I missed them, although not too much ... at that age.'

Parents and school chums were left behind, but the camaraderie of the tour bus made up for it. 'We'd all meet up at the bus depot at Allsop Place at the back of the Planetarium behind Marylebone. If you were there early you went for tea with the bus driver. That was the start of every tour. Later on, after I had moved to Hendon from Hackney, I used to pick up the coach at Hendon because it passed near the top of the road where I lived.'

Helen was still at school during her first year in the business. 'I was fourteen, but I was fortunate that I had an understanding headmistress. She would occasionally let me off for an afternoon to do *Parade Of The Pops* or some other show on the *Light Programme*. However, I was limited to what I could do in the school holidays at that stage.'

Helen was still a schoolgirl when she topped the bill at the Sunday Night At The London Palladium in October 1961:

It was such a thrill. It was the first time I'd played the Palladium and when I finished, the curtains opened, and the compère Bruce Forsyth came on to meet me to lead me on to the revolving circle and he said Welcome Home. It was very special. I was back behind my school desk the next morning. That's the sort of double life I led. It was funny because the press would sneak in to the school. You'd get a photographer shinning up a drainpipe to take a picture. It used to make the other kids laugh.

Concerts were reasonably rare during that first year: 'It was always cinemas. I had to close the first half because I was still at school and I had to be out by 10 p.m. – it was the law, I think. London County Council, as it still was then, would have to carry out inspections of the dressing room area. I don't know how some of those places passed!'

Helen finally left school in December 1961, just a couple of months after that first joyous Palladium date:

I had to leave school because I was making a film. I left two weeks before the end of term so I had to have a tutor for a couple of weeks – again by law.

I had my first three hits during my first year – *Don't Treat Me Like A Child*, *You Don't Know* and *Walkin' Back To Happiness*. Once I left school Arthur Howes got in touch with Norrie Paramor's brother Alan, who was my manager, to arrange my first pop package tour, and I was topping the bill. It was great. I couldn't wait to leave school and go full-time.

If there was such a thing as an overnight success, then Helen was it. There were advance orders of 300,000 for *Walkin' Back To Happiness*, her biggest hit yet.

Along with the UK tour there were international dates in far flung places like America, Canada, Australia and New Zealand. It sounds glamorous, but it was not quite the high life: 'Even for a kid like me it was pretty exhausting. There were no wide bodied jets in those days and I travelled tourist class, and there were up to six stop-overs on the way.'

Helen and the Beatles' paths were to cross from time to time, as was typical for pop stars in the smaller London of the 1960s. Occasionally, it might be in the Abbey Road recording studios they both used, like on one memorable occasion in 1964:

I was using studio 1 or 3 while the Beatles were recording *Can't Buy Me Love* in studio 2. So I decided to call in and it was great to see them. They came over and gave me a hug. Of course it was John who made a fuss of me and made me a cup of tea and did the big brother thing – though I didn't really see him as my big brother!

There were also several meetings on *Ready Steady Go*, including one where Helen mimed her song *Look Who It Is* to Paul, George, and Ringo, while John tried his utmost to make her giggle by pulling grotesque faces.

Helen finished touring at the end of 2002, after forty-two years in the business, to concentrate on Gospel outreach evenings.

She was at the funeral of Danny Williams, who died in December 2005: 'He died only about four or five weeks after he was diagnosed with lung cancer. Danny was always on my tours. He was a wonderful singer. He was known as the British Johnny Mathis, but I preferred Danny's voice.'

The Beatles do their best to look enthusiastic about yet another interview, this time before their appearance at the Ipswich Gaumont on Saturday 31 October 1964, on the Mary Wells tour. (*East Anglian Daily Times*)

The Beatles pop package tour dates and venues

2 FEBRUARY–3 MARCH 1963: **Helen Shapiro, Danny Williams, Kenny Lynch, the Beatles, the Red Price Band, the Honeys and the Kestrels. Compère: Dave Allen**

Saturday 2 February	Gaumont Cinema, Bradford
Tuesday 5 February	Gaumont Cinema, Doncaster
Wednesday 6 February	Granada Cinema, Bedford
Thursday 7 February	Regal Cinema in Wakefield, Yorkshire
Friday 8 February	ABC Cinema, Carlisle
Saturday 9 February	Empire Theatre, Sunderland

Tour break

Saturday 23 February	Gaumont Cinema, Mansfield
Sunday 24 February	Coventry Theatre
Tuesday 26 February	Gaumont Cinema, Taunton
Wednesday 27 February	Rialto Theatre, York
Thursday 28 February	Granada Cinema, Shrewsbury
Friday 1 March	Odeon Cinema, Southport
Saturday 2 March	City Hall, Sheffield
Sunday 3 March	Gaumont Cinema, Hanley

9 MARCH–31 MARCH 1963: **Chris Montez, Tommy Roe, the Terry Young Six, the Viscounts, Debbie Lee, the Beatles. Compère: Tony Marsh**

Saturday 9 March	Granada Cinema, East Ham
Sunday 10 March	Hippodrome Theatre, Birmingham
Tuesday 12 March	Granada Cinema, Bedford
Wednesday 13 March	Rialto Theatre, York
Thursday 14 March	Gaumont Cinema, Wolverhampton
Friday 15 March	Colston Hall, Bristol
Saturday 16 March	City Hall, Sheffield
Sunday 17 March	Embassy Cinema, Peterborough
Monday 18 March	Regal Cinema, Gloucester
Tuesday 19 March	Regal Cinema, Cambridge
Wednesday 20 March	ABC Cinema, Romford
Thursday 21 March	ABC Cinema, West Croydon
Friday 22 March	Gaumont Cinema, Doncaster
Saturday 23 March	City Hall, Newcastle
Sunday 24 March	Empire Theatre, Liverpool

'We love you yeah, yeah yeah…' Queuing to see the Beatles at the Gaumont Cinema in Ipswich. (*East Anglian Daily Times*)

Tuesday 26 March	Granada Cinema, Mansfield
Wednesday 27 March	ABC Cinema, Northampton
Thursday 28 March	ABC Cinema, Exeter
Friday 29 March	Odeon Cinema, Lewisham
Saturday 30 March	Guildhall, Portsmouth
Sunday 31 March	De Montfort Hall, Leicester

18 MAY–9 JUNE 1963: **Roy Orbison, the Beatles, Gerry and the Pacemakers, the Terry Young Six, Erkey Grant, Ian Crawford, David Macbeth and Louise Cordet. Compère: Tony Marsh**

Saturday 18 May	Adelphi Cinema, Slough
Sunday 19 May	Gaumont Cinema, Hanley
Monday 20 May	Gaumont Cinema, Southampton
Wednesday 22 May	Gaumont Cinema, Ipswich
Thursday 23 May	Odeon Cinema, Nottingham
Friday 24 May	Granada Cinema, Walthamstow
Saturday 25 May	City Hall, Sheffield
Sunday 26 May	Empire Theatre, Liverpool
Monday 27 May	Cardiff Capitol
Tuesday 28 May	Gaumont Cinema, Worcester
Wednesday 29 May	Rialto Theatre, York
Thursday 30 May	Odeon Cinema, Manchester
Friday 31 May	Odeon Cinema, Southend
Saturday 1 June	Granada Cinema, Tooting
Sunday 2 June	Hippodrome, Brighton
Monday 3 June	Granada Cinema, Woolwich
Tuesday 4 June	Town Hall, Birmingham
Wednesday 5 June	Odeon Cinema, Leeds
Friday 7 June	Odeon Cinema, Glasgow
Saturday 8 June	City Hall, Newcastle
Sunday 9 June	King George's Hall, Blackburn

1 NOVEMBER–13 DECEMBER 1963: **The Beatles, the Kestrels, Peter Jay and the Jaywalkers, the Vernons Girls, the Brook Brothers, the Rhythm and Blues Quartet. Compère: Frank Berry**

Friday 1 November	Odeon Cinema, Cheltenham
Saturday 2 November	City Hall, Sheffield
Sunday 3 November	Odeon Cinema, Leeds
Tuesday 5 November	Adelphi Cinema, Slough

The Colston Hall, Bristol, in 2006. This is actually the fourth Colston Hall, the previous three having been destroyed by fire. The current building is still a major venue and significant improvements are being planned. It was the scene of an uproarious finale to the Beatles tour on 10 November 1964, when students hiding up in the gantries emptied flour on the band as they sang. (Author's collection)

Sheffield City Hall staged its fair share of pop package concerts in the 1960s and it was still standing strong in 2006. (Stephen Brookes)

The Winter Gardens in Bournemouth, the scene of some 1963 Beatlemania. (Courtesy of Bournemouth Public Library with thanks to Jan Marsh)

Wednesday 6 November	ABC Cinema, Northampton
Thursday 7 November	Adelphi Cinema, Dublin
Friday 8 November	Ritz Cinema, Belfast
Saturday 9 November	Granada Cinema, East Ham
Sunday 10 November	Hippodrome, Birmingham
Wednesday 13 November	ABC Cinema, Plymouth
Thursday 14 November	ABC Cinema, Exeter
Friday 15 November	Colston Hall, Bristol
Saturday 16 November	Winter Gardens Theatre, Bournemouth
Sunday 17 November	Coventry Theatre
Tuesday 19 November	Gaumont Cinema, Wolverhampton
Wednesday 20 November	ABC Cinema, Manchester
Thursday 21 November	ABC Cinema, Carlisle
Friday 22 November	Globe Cinema, Stockton-on-Tees, Durham
Saturday 23 November	City Hall, Newcastle
Sunday 24 November	ABC Cinema, Hull
Tuesday 26 November	Regal Cinema, Cambridge
Wednesday 27 November	Rialto Theatre, York
Thursday 28 November	ABC Cinema, Lincoln
Friday 29 November	ABC Cinema, Huddersfield
Saturday 30 November	Empire Theatre, Sunderland
Sunday 1 December	De Montfort Hall, Leicester
Tuesday 3 December	Guildhall, Portsmouth
(Postponed from Tuesday 12 November)	
Saturday 7 December	Odeon Cinema, Liverpool
Sunday 8 December	Odeon Cinema, Lewisham

Monday 9 December	Odeon Cinema, Southend
Tuesday 10 December	Gaumont Cinema, Doncaster
Wednesday 11 December	Futurist Theatre, Scarborough
Thursday 12 December	Odeon Cinema, Nottingham
Friday 13 December	Gaumont Cinema, Southampton

9 OCTOBER–10 NOVEMBER 1964: **The Beatles, Mary Wells, Sounds Incorporated, Tommy Quickly, the Remo Four and the Rustiks. Compère: Bob Bain**

Friday 9 October	Gaumont Cinema, Bradford
Saturday 10 October	De Montfort Hall, Leicester
Sunday 11 October	Odeon Cinema, Birmingham
Tuesday 13 October	ABC Cinema, Wigan
Wednesday 14 October	ABC Cinema, Manchester
Thursday 15 October	Globe Cinema, Stockton-on-Tees
Friday 16 October	ABC Cinema, Hull
Monday 19 October	ABC Cinema, Edinburgh
Tuesday 20 October	Caird Hall, Dundee
Wednesday 21 October	Odeon Cinema, Glasgow
Thursday 22 October	Odeon Cinema, Leeds
Friday 23 October	Gaumont State Cinema, Kilburn
Saturday 24 October	Granada Cinema, Walthamstow
Sunday 25 October	Hippodrome, Brighton
Wednesday 28 October	ABC Cinema, Exeter

Thursday 29 October	ABC Cinema, Plymouth
Friday 30 October	Gaumont Cinema, Bournemouth
Saturday 31 October	Gaumont Cinema, Ipswich
Sunday 1 November	Astoria Cinema, Finsbury Park
Monday 2 November	King's Hall, Belfast
Wednesday 4 November	Ritz Cinema, Luton
Thursday 5 November	Odeon Cinema, Nottingham
Friday 6 November	Gaumont Cinema, Southampton
Saturday 7 November	Capitol Cinema, Cardiff
Sunday 8 November	Empire Theatre, Liverpool
Monday 9 November	City Hall, Sheffield
Tuesday 10 November	Colston Hall, Bristol

3 DECEMBER–12 DECEMBER 1965: **The Beatles, the Moody Blues, the Paramounts, the Koobas, Beryl Marsden, Steve Aldo**

Friday 3 December	Odeon Cinema, Glasgow
Saturday 4 December	City Hall, Newcastle
Sunday 5 December	Empire Theatre, Liverpool
Tuesday 7 December	ABC Cinema, Manchester
Wednesday 8 December	Gaumont Cinema, Sheffield
Thursday 9 December	Odeon Cinema, Birmingham
Friday 10 December	Odeon Cinema, Hammersmith
Saturday 11 December	Astoria Cinema, Finsbury Park
Sunday 12 December	Capitol Cinema, Cardiff

Two

The Del Shannon Tour

When Del boy rocked the old ABC

THE FINAL CURTAIN fell on the ABC Cinema in Aldershot's High Street on Thursday 10 July 2003, after sixty-six years of bringing the latest films to the town.

It was also the scene of teenage hysteria in the 1960s when a whole host of stars appeared there in a series of pop supershows, featuring names such as Del Shannon, Roy Orbison, the Kinks, and the Small Faces.

These were the days when the biggest names in the pop world were not too proud to appear in clubs and cinemas in your High Street. Hit Parade rivals often toured together, giving fans the ear-splitting opportunity to out-scream each other and on one amazing tour the Walker Brothers, Jimi Hendrix, Engelbert Humperdinck and Cat Stevens all appeared on the same show!

The Aldershot gigs were typical. The show would hit town for one night only, featuring two performances, one at 6.15 p.m. and one at 8.30 p.m. Aldershot's first, on Tuesday 16 March 1965, starring American sensation Del Shannon, was an unqualified success. Stalls and circle tickets (6s 6d, 8s 6d and 10s 6d) went on sale from Saturday 13 February and were snapped up in a matter of days.

Hordes of screaming teenagers broke through police barriers as the twenty-six-year-old Shannon arrived at the cinema that afternoon, and when the exhausted idol left after the two shows his chauffeur-driven Cadillac was given a police escort away from the baying fans.

Del's lavish spending was not limited to his cars. His mink guitar strap set him back a cool $125 – almost as much as the guitar. He could afford it. He had already made his money from a string of hits and he had invested in stocks and shares – and several oil wells!

Two lucky girls get their up-close moment with Peter Noone at the Gaumont in Ipswich.

Del was on something of a revival. His latest song, *Keep Searchin'*, had reached number three in the UK charts and he was in an upbeat mood when he spoke to the music press on the eve of the tour. It kicked off at the City Hall, Sheffield, on Saturday 27 February, to rave reviews and finished, twenty-one dates later, at the Odeon Glasgow on 22 March.

Shannon ran through a succession of his hits on that opening night in Yorkshire. He kicked off with *Hey Little Girl* and then got the falsetto voice really rolling for *Hats Off To Larry*, followed by *Swiss Maid, Little Town Flirt, Runaway* and the Gene Pitney song *I'm Gonna Be Strong*. Del then announced *Keep Searchin'* with the words, 'Here's a tune that's been good to me lately'. He left the stage, but returned to big applause and the final number, *Stranger In Town*.

The up-and-coming Herman's Hermits, featuring a toothy seventeen-year-old singer called Peter Noone, were the back-up stars, but they were getting at least as many screams. They selected *I'm Into Something Good, Can't You Hear My Heartbeat, End Of The World, Silhouettes*, which had hit the charts a few days before and was still climbing, and *Mrs Brown You've Got A Lovely Daughter*. This number had actually been offered to Joe Brown, but he had turned it down, a decision he was later to lament when he realised how successful it was. Noone, with his trademark grin, went on to wow American girls with the song when the group performed it on the Ed Sullivan Show.

Wayne Fontana and the Mindbenders were also on the package and they had a couple of big numbers to bring to the party. *Um Um Um Um Um Um* and *Game Of Love* were smash hits for the band and Wayne added a couple of classic rockers – *High Heel Sneakers* and *Too Much*

Top Artists Fly B O A C

AN
ABC
THEATRE

ABC - ALDERSHOT

Manager: P. Jackson   Telephone: 20355

ONE DAY ONLY   ON THE STAGE   TWO PERFORMANCES ONLY
(instead of the usual film programme)

TUES.. 16th MARCH at 6.15 & 8.30

Peter Walsh, Kennedy Street Enterprises Ltd. and Tito Burns present

FROM THE U.S.A.
DEL SHANNON
'KEEP SEARCHIN'

HIT PARADE STARS
WAYNE FONTANA and the MINDBENDERS
'THE GAME OF LOVE'

HERMAN'S HERMITS
— SILHOUETTES —

JUST FOUR MEN | **PAUL DEAN** | **THE SOUL SAVAGES** | **JERRY STEVENS**

guest stars from America
The SHANGRI-LAS
'Leader of the pack'

TICKETS   Stalls & Circle   10/6   8/6   6/6
ALL SEATS BOOKABLE IN ADVANCE

POSTAL BOOKING FORM—DEL SHANNON   Date ....
To the BOX OFFICE, ABC THEATRE, ALDERSHOT   Please forward .... stalls/circle at ....
For the 6.15/8.30 performance on Tuesday, 16th March
enclose stamped addressed envelope and P.O./Cheque value   £ .... s. .... d.
(Please delete words not applicable)
Name .... Address ....

A rare handbill, rescued by the cinema staff, from the Del Shannon 1965 tour.

Monkey Business, plus *One More Time* to bring the crowd to their feet as they closed the first half.

Special guest Twinkle, looking stunning in a full-length blue satin gown, delighted the audience on that memorable opening night, contributing *Roll Over Beethoven*, *Oh Boy*, her big hit, *Terry*, and her new single *Golden Lights*.

The Dollies, four girls who had left school a matter of weeks before, made their mark with their version of *Walkin' The Dog*, while the Just Four Men played safe with *La Bamba*. Del, Twinkle and the Dollies were all backed by the Soul Savages. The Savages did not go on to earn rock 'n' roll immortality, but their organist on the tour, a talented young hopeful called Paul Nicholas, later made quite a name for himself as an actor and singer.

After that dazzling opening night the show moved swiftly on to the Liverpool Empire the next night and then the Town Hall, Birmingham, the Gaumont at Wolverhampton and the Odeon in Manchester.

It was the usual pattern of mayhem all around. The screams were at full pitch inside and outside the Wolverhampton venue, with Fontana and Noone attracting even more than the bill-topper. Del certainly went down well, though, finishing his spot with *Keep Searchin'* and *I'm Gonna Be Strong*. Twinkle was also in good form, with *Roll Over Beethoven* catching the ear of the local reporter.

The American girl group, the Shangri-Las, joined the package on fifteen of the twenty-one dates, including that final night in Glasgow. The girls were featuring their big song, *Leader Of The Pack*, which was in the charts at the time. They also threw in *Give Him A Great Big Kiss* and *Shout*.

After the Manchester show, the tour enjoyed a night off before heading up to Scotland for dates at the Aberdeen Capitol on Friday 5 March and the Dundee Caird Hall the following night, with a show at the Newcastle City Hall finishing off the week.

On Tuesday 9 March they headed off to the ABC Cinema at Northampton, the first of six successive shows in the unrelenting schedule. From there it was straight off to the Salisbury Odeon, the ABC Cinema in Dover, the Lewisham Odeon, the Odeon at Colchester and the Hammersmith Commodore.

Everywhere they went they were running the gauntlet. Noone told the *NME* he was nursing an injured thumb that a policeman managed to shut in a taxi door as they made a desperate bid for freedom from the screaming hordes at Hammersmith. He was also risking the wrath of Twinkle's mum, having kept the teen out until 3 a.m., courtesy of a bit of partying at the Ad Lib Club in London.

They had the Monday off to recover before playing the ABC Cinema in Aldershot but, as on so many tours, the hectic pace was creating casualties. The Shangri-Las had to cry off from Aldershot due to the illness of their lead singer. Their spot was filled by Dodie West, who had already had a minor hit with *I Think I'm Going Out Of My Head*.

Another star who did not make it as far as Aldershot was Wayne Fontana and so the Mindbenders had to gamely battle on without him. It was reported that Wayne had collapsed with exhaustion the previous Wednesday when the tour reached Salisbury. He went home to Manchester to recuperate, with his father telling the music press that his son needed a break.

In fact, it was even more serious. Wayne had suffered a breakdown and he took no further part in the tour. Nobody saw it coming. Wayne and Peter Noone, who had known each other for several years, had been having great fun. There was plenty of boyish humour as they dived in and out of each other's dressing rooms, playing tricks on each other, and then there was the socialising after the shows. Noone told a reporter, 'We usually go off to a club or restaurant then return to our hotel and sit drinking coffee and talking to the small hours.'

Looking back in January 2005, he had a more realistic assessment as he recalled the excesses of those early days on the road. He said:

Wow, I actually remember Wayne missing that show! Wayne and I still work every time I tour the UK, which is every two years. He was having trouble staying away from P.J. Proby and all the other losers out there then. Oops, they are still out there! For some unknown reason, we all thought that being able to out-drink each other was part of the road warrior's armour.

Fortunately, being the youngest, I won every night, and live to tell the tale with some lucidity. Never missed a concert. Never fell off a stage. Sold 80 million records and still do 150 concerts a year. I have a thirty-year mortgage so expect to see me back in Aldershot some day. I'm alive and well and living the high life in Santa Barbara, California, on a golf course on which I have never played and never intend to [Birnam Wood]. By the way, have they cleaned the dressing rooms yet?

That question is academic, as the old Aldershot Cinema is no more.

The Zephyrs had been immediately drafted in as replacements for Wayne on that fateful night in Salisbury. Brian Poole and Eden Kane filled in on two other nights. Shannon, backed by the Soul Savages, was still in good voice, and he received that amazing reception from the Aldershot fans.

There was great excitement during the whole of both Aldershot shows. Stewards and St John Ambulance volunteers were kept busy dealing with tearful girls trying to storm the stage. Shannon went through his repertoire of hits to a backdrop of screams, with *Stranger In Town*, *I'm Gonna Be Strong* and *Keep Searchin'* all earning a mention in coverage by the *Aldershot News*.

I'm Into Something Good and *Silhouettes* drew a particularly excited response for Herman's Hermits. The Zombies came in for Aldershot and they included the Righteous Brothers' hit *You've Lost That Loving Feeling*, plus one of their own songs, *She's Coming Home*, in their set.

She's Not There had been a decent hit for them the previous summer, reaching number twelve, and they were hoping these dates would prove a launching pad for their latest offering, *Tell Her No*. Sadly, the song peaked at a modest number forty-two and was spending its final week in the charts as the show hit Aldershot.

The Just Four Men got a rousing reception when they performed *La Bamba* and their latest record *There's Not One Thing*. The Dollies took their moment in the spotlight, delighting the Aldershot audience with their version of *Goodnight Baby*. The twenty-year-old Belgian-born singer Paul Dean completed the line-up.

The compère for the tour was Jerry Stevens who, true to the traditions of the 1960s pop show, kept the teenagers entertained with his lively patter – not to mention passable mimics of television comic Charlie Drake and cartoon favourite Yogi Bear!

The Ivy League had joined the tour the day before as special guests. They were already enjoying some success as their song *Can't You Hear*

(*Above*) **The young Julia Clarke pictured in the 1960s.** (Courtesy of Julia Clarke)

(*Above right*) **Julia Clarke pictured by the author with her daughter Anna.**

My Heartbeat? had been a hit in the US for Herman's Hermits, and in the UK with Goldie and the Gingerbreads. Better still, they had a current Top Ten smash of their own, *Funny How Love Can Be*, which had entered the charts on 4 February and was to remain there for nine weeks.

Of course, the Aldershot ABC's first tentative step into the pop world was greeted with joy by its young audience. All these years later, fans still have clear memories of the excitement of it all.

Julia Clarke, in those days fourteen-year-old Julia Hill, a pupil of St Michael's School in Aldershot, recalls Peter Noone's trademark non-stop clapping as he sang *I'm Into Something Good*; this despite him telling music writer Penny Valentine the previous month that he was giving it up because of the blisters on his hands! Julia's account was backed up by the *NME*, which recorded Noone's clapping on the opening night, despite the blisters.

Julia said:

I went along with two school friends, Susan Green and Rona Warriner. We were in the end class and went around together. I remember him clapping throughout *I'm Into Something Good*, just as he did on the television. I mainly went to see Del Shannon as he had a couple of big hits, and *Runaway* was particularly good. But he was one of those who didn't look so good in the flesh. The groups did look good though, especially Herman's Hermits.

I liked the Zombies too because of *She's Not There*. Somebody in the audience shouted a request for it, but they didn't play it. I was disappointed about that, but maybe they didn't have time.

I remember having a sort of fluttering sound in my ears for days afterwards because everything was so loud – especially Del Shannon. But then it all had to be loud to get over the screaming. It wasn't just at the end of each song, it was all through the songs as well. No wonder my ears were ringing for days. I don't think I would have screamed – I'm not really that type – but I'm sure we would have joined in the cheering. We had only seen them on the TV before and of course they were big news.

I lived on the Heronwood estate in those days and would have gone to the early evening show, travelling there and back on the bus. The father of one of the other girls worked at the fish shop almost opposite the cinema, so I expect we persuaded him to get the tickets for us beforehand. We certainly didn't queue up on the night.

It was the only pop show Julia, who now lives just a few miles away in Ash, recalls attending at the ABC but she certainly saw plenty of the nearby Odeon Cinema. She became the projectionist there for nine years!

Another person at that opening show was Mick Redfern, in those days a seventeen-year-old apprentice baker at Brickells where the High Street joins Ash Road. Mick, who now lives in the nearby village of Normandy, said:

In those days I earned the princely sum of one shilling one and a ha'penny an hour so the entrance fee was a lot of money to me. I had to pick and choose carefully when I went out.

The thing I remember most is my mate Paul King, who now lives on the Isle of Wight, being in the Pegasus pub opposite the cinema immediately before the show when Peter Noone came in. Paul asked him for an autograph, but the only thing he had for him to sign was a ten bob note, so he got him to sign that.

I was already in my seat in the ABC by then. When Paul came in he was quite excited about it. He swore that he would never spend that ten bob, but I know full well that he did. It was just too much money.

I thoroughly enjoyed the whole thing – having pop stars that close to you. It just didn't happen. You had only seen these guys on the telly before. I remember Peter Noone almost getting dragged off stage by a couple of girls. Del Shannon was great of course – I really enjoyed seeing him.

And the coolest job of all? That award goes to sixteen-year-old Patricia Pittock and a group of her mates from Woolworth's who not only got in for free, but got paid too. Patricia and her pals were invited to sell ice creams at the first two Aldershot shows, headlined respectively by Del Shannon and the Kinks.

Patricia got a glimpse of her idol Peter Noone afterwards while waiting for a lift home: 'My friend's dad was due to pick us up and we were standing at the front of the cinema when we spotted him with some other men on the opposite side of the road. I don't know who the others were – they might even have been group members, but we were too shy to shout out or go over for an autograph.'

The success of that opening show was very good news for Peter Jackson, who had come up from Hove in Sussex just two weeks before to manage the Aldershot cinema. He said at the time, 'This is the first pop show we have had, although there have been others in nearby towns. I am sure we will try to get more. It is just the sort of entertainment the young people like.'

He proved to be as good as his word. Just a few weeks later, on Wednesday 5 May, chart sensations the Kinks topped the bill on the second pop show at the ABC.

As for the stars on this tour, they still had another six successive nights to survive. From Aldershot the package set off for the Taunton Gaumont the next night and then on to the Worcester Gaumont, the Leeds Odeon, the Bolton Odeon and the Hanley Gaumont before the last – hurrah – all the way up in Scotland at the Glasgow Odeon.

Pranks and the occasional séance – life on the road

They may have been called the Hermits, but there was nothing hermit-like about the lifestyle of Peter Noone and his mates on that 1965 British tour.

Barry Whitwam, who is still the group's drummer today, said:

We had a great time. We were basically still kids and we used to get up to all sorts of pranks. There were thirty-odd people on the tour bus and we must have been a right handful. One day we got some peashooters and were firing peas at one another and making a hell of a racket. When the driver pulled up anywhere all these peas would go hurtling along the floor towards him. You should have heard it.

We used to trash each other's dressing rooms, of course. My party piece was to hang up all the chairs on coat hooks until one of the Mindbenders' roadies caught me. He hung my jacket up on a coat hook with me still in it and I was stuck there for about half an hour!

Among the playful banter, was something of a darker nature – the occasional séance:

Derek Leckenby and I started it when I was about fourteen and Derek eighteen, before we were even in the Hermits. There would

Although there were plenty of pranks, there was not a complete lack of discipline:

Our tour manager was Fred Perry – the same name as the tennis player. He was a good bloke, but he had this rule that the coach wouldn't wait any longer than 60 seconds. After that, it was off and you missed it. Two of the boys got left in Scotland once and they had a 12-hour train journey to get down to the gig in Somerset. They arrived with just minutes to spare. I learned punctuality then, and it has never left me to this day.

It did rebound on Fred once, though. He got left behind himself when he was late. The coach pulled away as he came running up the road and we didn't stop. He didn't take it well!

Bill-topper Del Shannon was popular with his fellow musicians, even if he was making his own way to gigs in his chauffeur-driven Cadillac.

'He was a great guy,' said Whitwam. 'We would all have a drink together at the hotel after the gigs and talk and drink the night away until the porters slung us out so they could close up. Del liked the English beer.'

However, the traditional last-night prank tested the American's humour: 'One of the lads lengthened Del's guitar strap. When he went on stage to sing the first number it was hanging down by his knees. He wasn't amused by that! He explained to the audience that someone had played a trick on him, but he wasn't happy.'

Herman's Hermits were workaholics during that period. Whitwam recalled:

We were having the time of our lives, but it was mayhem. From Christmas 1964 until 1966 we had just three days off. We did three month-long UK tours in 1965 – plus America. We also made a film. And that's not even mentioning TV work and making records.

On the telly, we appeared on everything from *Sooty* and *Crackerjack* to *Top Of The Pops*. When we went to America, it was just mad. We did 100 TV and radio shows in two weeks, from New York to California. We would just pick up our instruments, mime to our songs and then it was straight off to the next one.

Of course, as much as the adulation from the girls was welcome, it could sometimes get out of hand. 'There were occasions when you had to run for your life,' said Whitwam. 'If you got trapped, you were in trouble. The girls would be coming at us with scissors trying to cut off locks of our hair. If we weren't quick on our feet we could have been bald!'

Like many 1960s groups, Herman's Hermits did not benefit as much as they should have from all that hard work.

Despite all that, Whitwam is not still playing today because he has to, he's playing because he loves to. 'It's in my blood. It's what I do,' he said. 'The excitement of being up on stage and hearing the applause of

be about five or six of us, all gathered around the table with the glass, the usual stuff.

Eventually, Derek and I stopped doing it after we had a bit of a fright. There were four of us in the room and there was a piano and the glass was going crazy pointing at the answers Yes and No, Yes and No. Then all of a sudden the full chord of C came out of the piano – really powerfully – and there was nobody within ten feet of it. It frightened us to death and we stopped doing it after that.

Although drummer Whitwam and guitarist Leckenby had learned their lesson, some of the other Manchester lads on that 1965 tour were all too willing to take a chance. 'Wayne Fontana was holding a séance in a room with the Just Four Men. All of a sudden the guitarist got up and crushed the glass in his hand, cutting his veins. They stopped it after that,' said Barry.

Barry Whitwam, seated, with the Hermits in 2006. (Courtesy of Barry Whitwam)

the audience, everyone on their feet, is why we do it. It's just as much fun now as it was back then. It's a great life where you never really have to grow up!'

Herman's Hermits' line-up in those days was Peter Noone (vocals), Derek Leckenby (guitar), Keith Hopwood (guitar), Karl Green (bass) and Barry Whitwam (drums). The Zombies were Colin Blunstone (vocals), Rod Argent (keyboards), Paul Arnold (bass), Hugh Grundy (drums) and Paul Atkinson (guitar). The Mindbenders were made up of Ric Rothwell (drums), Eric Stewart (guitar and vocals), Bob Lang (bass), and the Just Four Men were Demetrius Christopholus (guitar and vocals), Lally Scott (guitar), Keith Sheppard (bass) and Lawrence Arends (drums).

When the Beatles & Stones rolled into Wayne's world

When the Beatles and the Stones had engagements in Manchester they were lucky to have an old pal who could guide them to the city's hottest and most discreet nightclubs so they could let their hair down away from the prying eyes and ears of the media.

Wayne Fontana and the Fabs' friendship dated back to the sweaty, leather-jacketed, pre-fame days when the Beatles arrived back home from their Hamburg stints. Wayne recalled:

We often played the same venues in those days. They were brilliant guys, all of them. John was difficult to get to know, but when you had earned his trust he was a wonderful friend. Because I knew them before they were famous there wasn't this suspicion they had for people who suddenly wanted to be around them for some sort of reflected glory.

We first got to know them when they got back from Germany and were playing at the famous Oasis Club in Manchester. My management owned the club at the time. The Beatles used to leave all sorts of things behind in the Oasis. They would forget them – wonderful things like the corduroy jackets they used to wear, and scarves. If I'd known then what I know now. Can you imagine owning a whole set of Beatle corduroy jackets and scarves from the early 1960s? What would they be worth today?

We did a gig with them in Stoke-on-Trent when the neck broke off John's Rickenbacker. He simply broke it up and dumped it in a bin. I'd have grabbed that too if I had known.

The shared passion for music was a basis for firm friendships between the budding pop stars of Merseyside and Manchester in a way that would horrify their football counterparts. 'There was no

animosity between Manchester and Liverpool bands,' said Wayne. 'We got on very well together, although I'd say that there were actually far more bands in Manchester than Liverpool. The Merseybeat thing was mainly because of the Beatles, but there was a huge and exciting scene in Manchester.'

Wayne didn't just play host to the Fabs. He was also mates with their great rivals, the Rolling Stones. London boys Jagger and Richards knew even less about the Manchester scene than the Beatles, but Wayne was more than happy to help them out:

They were the same, Mick and Keith, really great blokes, and I really looked after them. I took them to Belle Vue Zoo and showed them around the Kings Hall before their gig there that night. Mick had forgotten his harmonica so I drove all the way back to the Oasis so he could use mine. The Oasis was the place to go in Manchester and we'd all make a beeline for it after the show. They were marvellous, the Stones. Brian Jones was a great guy too.

Wayne was a star in his own right, with *Game Of Love* topping charts all over the world (apart from the UK where it was kept off the top spot by the Seekers), but even he was daunted by the Beatles. 'It was a strange feeling. There was I, a Top Ten pop star, but I was just as awed as any other fan in their presence. I'm touring with P.J. Proby at this moment and it's a similar feeling. I've idolised him for years and now I'm on tour with him and he's up there singing all my favourites.'

Having just one hit single in the 1960s could get you instant top billing over stars whose flame had been burning considerably longer. 'After *Game Of Love* was a hit I went over to America as the top of the bill – above Jerry Lee Lewis, the Shirelles and Fats Domino. It was ridiculous, and all on the strength of just one hit. It felt amazing, but it was sick really. These people were massive. I just wonder what they must have thought.'

Wayne also recalls that fateful night of the Del Shannon/Herman's Hermits tour in 1965 when he succumbed to the pressure of being a workaholic pop star:

I had a breakdown. That's the way to describe it. We were on our way to Salisbury for a gig there that night. I felt suddenly really strange. It was as if I was in a different world. I had this incredible fear. It wasn't stage fright – it was just anxiety, a fear of everything, like a panic attack. We didn't know then what we know now about depression and such things, but it hit me very suddenly and I couldn't go on. I just wanted to get back home to Manchester to be with my parents. That was all I wanted. So I got in the car, and the journey seemed to take forever. God knows how I managed to drive like that, but I did get home.

Wayne could not rejoin the tour and it was many months before he recovered enough to resume his pop career:

Looking back at the pictures from those 1960s tours, Wayne wonders how the fans heard anything over the screams. 'We would have several guitars, plus the bass and microphones all coming out of one amp. It must have sounded awful. Look at the pictures. There's hardly any gear on stage. Not a monitor in sight and certainly no mixing desks. It was all just so basic.'

If the gear was basic, the accommodation and pay was worse than basic. 'The most we ever got paid was £350 and we only saw £130 out of that, and that had to go four ways. All the rest went to our agents for management fees. Then we had to pay our own expenses for accommodation. It all came out of it. That's why we ended up staying in such grubby places. Most of the time it would be all four of us crammed into one bedroom.'

Wayne enjoyed the company of Del Shannon on the 1965 tour:

He was a great performer and a good writer too. We became great friends. He was a nice, normal down to earth fella, but he did like a drink and that's what probably did for him in the end. I liked the Americans who came over. They were gentlemen. Roy Orbison. He was quiet, but a real gentleman. He would be happy to talk to you.

He used to collect cars. He'd be on the coach and if he saw a Roller or something and he fancied it he would get the coach to stop and he'd go over and talk to the guy and make him an offer. He'd arrange to have it shipped over to America. He was such a great talent too. On stage he would hardly move his mouth when he sang, but the fantastic sound that came out...

The Americans were better company than most of the Brits, who thought they were God's gift. A lot of the Brits were not much more than kids themselves – eighteen or nineteen and with giant egos. They thought they were the bees knees. Like that story of the Small Faces and the Hollies rowing over who was topping the bill. What was that all about? the Americans never behaved like that. They were far more professional and just got on with the job.

I never did fully recover from it. Nobody knew about severe depression then. Even my doctor didn't. He had this nice little cottage in the country and he said 'Why don't you go off there for a couple of weeks?' When I got back playing I began to drink to suppress it all and then the drink took hold and I eventually became an alcoholic.

Wayne Fontana, pictured on stage at the Anvil, Basingstoke, in 2006. (Author's collection)

Happily, when Wayne joined the Solid Silver Sixties tour in 2006 with P.J., Dave Dee, Dozy, Beaky, Mick and Tich, and Gerry and the Pacemakers he was enjoying life and had been off the bottle for twenty-three years. However, sadly Wayne has recently found himself involved in trouble with the law.

His friendship with Peter Noone, which predated that 1965 tour by several years, has stood the test of time and the pair still keep in touch, although Noone now lives on the west coast of America. 'He's a great mate,' said Wayne. 'Whenever we meet he always says he's my greatest fan. He comes over to tour and I always look forward to meeting up.'

Though touring is as tough as ever, with Britain's increasingly gridlocked roads, Wayne is enjoying his professional life. 'To be honest, I'd be doing this whether I got paid or not. I just love what I do,' he said. 'If I just had a normal job I'm sure I'd be doing this kind of thing in the evenings because I'm just a born entertainer. It's what I love doing.'

Like Hermits drummer Barry Whitwam, Wayne recalls the fascination for séances:

They did go on, it was a thing with the groups for a while, but I don't know what it was all about. Some of the guys would be taking the piss out of it, moving the glass around and all that, but Allan Clarke of the Hollies got up one night and ran straight into a glass door. That freaked me out and I stopped after that. The guys used to muck about, but this was different. I was on the Del Shannon tour at the time and the Hollies, who were on a different tour, were staying in the same hotel.

Overall, they were wonderful days. Just look at the pictures of Jimi Hendrix and Cat Stevens in the dressing room and on stage. Priceless. You wouldn't think there was anything left that hadn't already been snapped up and published.

Let me talk to Cat, I'm his fan club secretary!

Kathie Wilkins was handily placed for the pop nights at the Aldershot Cinema – she was a cashier at the Thomas Whites department store right opposite.

Kathie, who was not yet sixteen, was at the very first show in March 1965, when Del Shannon topped the bill, and she saw Jimi Hendrix when he strolled into the store two years later when the Experience came to town.

She distinguished herself that day by telephoning the cinema and demanding, as the secretary of his local fan club, to speak to Cat Stevens. Sadly for her the cinema staff were not to fall for such a ruse. She recalled with a smile:

It's the sort of thing I would get up to. I kept saying to the girls at work that I needed to talk to him. I wanted to know if he'd arrived. I said I'm going to ring them. The others said the cinema people wouldn't tell me anything and I said they would if I told them I'm the fan club secretary and we need to know if he's arrived yet.

I did ring, but they said he hadn't arrived. I tried to make it sound genuine by saying sombrely that he should have arrived by now. Then somebody said that Jimi Hendrix had been seen wandering around the town. I saw him on the corner outside Thomas Whites, but then he came in the store.

I worked on the third floor, but when word got out I went down to the ground floor and saw him. His clothes were really loud. He had orange striped trousers – certainly bright. I just thought, that's Jimi Hendrix. Fine. Then I went back upstairs to work.

Thomas Whites was an old-fashioned store with a reputation in the town, and senior staff would have frowned on the younger ones stopping work to try to get a glimpse of pop stars, but it did not deter high-spirited Kathie – now Kathie Soane – from trying to lead them astray.

Kathie had become head cashier in accounts by then, but her young charges were teasing her as she stirred up the excitement. She recalled:

The funny thing is, I didn't go to the show after all that. I was still only earning £3 something a week and I had other things to spend my money on I suppose. Having been to the first ABC show two years earlier I probably thought I had done that now.

Kathie is convinced that one of her friends would have organised the tickets for the one show she did go to, featuring Herman's Hermits, the Zombies, Dodie West, plus the Mindbenders, as well as bill-topper Del Shannon:

It wouldn't have been me. I was a bit lazy so I would probably have delegated that to one of the others. But we definitely went upstairs, because it was cheaper.

However, that Del Shannon show was to cost Kathie more than the 6s 6d for her seat:

I had one of those long blue chiffon scarves that you would wear in a car with the roof down to keep your hair in place. But we all stood up and started to throw things as we got carried away and I lobbed my scarf at Del Shannon – and, of course, that was the last I saw of it. It was only later when you thought to yourself 'Oh no, I could have worn that today'. Because you're fifteen, you don't care. It was easy come, easy go. You had no responsibility.

Kathie's verdict on the show?

I loved the music. It was loud, but the screaming was even louder. I doubt if anyone could have heard much, but that didn't matter. I would have been screaming too. I knew all the songs at that time, but you would just hear the introduction and the rest would be lost to a wail of screaming and cheering.

Del Shannon may have been topping the bill, but he was not the top heartthrob for Kathie. She was looking forward to seeing Wayne Fontana and the Mindbenders – so she would have been disappointed when Wayne failed to appear:

Although I liked Del Shannon's music, he wasn't a screamable idol. Having said that, I would still be screaming, just because he was there!
Peter Noone was another favourite, so him being there would have been good.

Kathie, who still lives in Aldershot today, just a couple of streets from the then family home in Belle Vue Road, was

Kathie Soane, then Kathie Wilkins, pictured in the 1960s. (Courtesy of Kathie Soane)

Kathie Soane pictured by the author in 2006.

later to rub shoulders with another household name who graced the stage of the old ABC:

I was working in London in the late 1960s and a friend and I were hitchhiking one night. This car pulled over and we presumed it was for us, so we jumped in the back. We were all cocky, saying 'thank you James' to the chauffeur and we were chatty and full of it and then I saw this other guy and said 'Oh my God, you're Gene Pitney. They took it all in good heart. Gene was in one corner at the back, with us taking up all the room, but he was very nice and friendly – a gentleman. Knowing me, I would probably have started singing to him. God, how embarrassing! They dropped us off where we wanted to go and at least I had the good grace to thank them.

All write on the night as the stars signed

These days, Kevin Hobbs and Tony Booth are near neighbours and mates in Farnborough, with music a key part of that friendship, but they barely knew each other in the 1960s when the stars came to play in Aldershot. They can, however, now reminisce about the days when the leading lights of the pop world descended on their local cinema.

It was the American stars who cut the mustard with Tony, who saw the first two shows at the ABC – starring Del Shannon and the Kinks. Tony, whose family home was in Camberley, was a sixteen-year-old apprentice technician at Marconi in Frimley:

Del Shannon and Duane Eddy were my heroes. I saw Duane at the Agincourt in Camberley and would have been excited about the prospect of seeing Del Shannon live.

When he came to Aldershot he hadn't had a hit in quite a while, but then all of a sudden *Keep Searchin'* rocketed into the charts.

I probably went by train. There was an easy route from Frimley to Aldershot – and I went to the later show. Among the songs were *Runaway* and *Keep Searchin'*, but only the slightly older people in the audience knew the old hits because it had been a couple of years since he had been high in the charts.

There must have been screaming, but I could hear him singing clearly and I contrast that with

Tony Booth and Kevin Hobbs pictured by the author in 2006.

when I saw the Rolling Stones a couple of times and couldn't hear anything for the screaming.

Del Shannon was brilliant, but the rest of that show I wasn't bothered about. I was a bit disappointed that Wayne Fontana wasn't there. The Zombies were good, though.

Tony owned a scooter, but did not class himself as a mod, and also has memories of the second show:

There was lots of screaming for the Walker Brothers, but it was the Kinks who I really went to see. They did *You Really Got Me* and *Tired Of Waiting* and *All Day And All Of The Night*. Some people didn't like them – thought they were a bit of a three-chord band, but I thought they were great and they were the reason I went. I remember Goldie and the Gingerbreads being on too.

Kevin is three years younger than Tony and was thirteen when he attended those first shows in 1965. He had one important advantage: his dad was in the army and he lived in military accommodation just over the road from the cinema! 'Dad was a saxophone player in the 2 Para band so I suppose I got my love of music from him. But he wasn't keen on the pop stuff. Turn it down, he would say.'

Kevin was at quite a few of the ABC shows and he was not shy about hanging around the stage door for autographs:

I vividly remember Goldie and the Gingerbreads from that second show. I was waiting in the car park afterwards when they came out and I asked 'Which one's Goldie?' One of them said 'I am'. I had a chat with her and she had a picture of the group they were giving out and she signed it for me. She was very pleasant. You could tell she enjoyed meeting the fans.

Roy Orbison, at his 1967 show, was another who signed:

I met Roy in the car park and he was a lovely bloke – really friendly. I had an autograph book that mum and dad gave me and he signed it and we chatted. Whenever you asked for an autograph at Aldershot, they were always obliging.

Engelbert gave me his autograph too in the car park. I used to hang around near the side door and I saw him get into his car. The stars always had people with them – managers and agents.

Kevin would attend the early evening shows – 'I can't see my mum letting me go to the later ones' – and Cat Stevens is prominent in the memories:

I remember him strapping on the holster for *I'm Gonna Get Me A Gun*. That was really good – the cowboy stuff. Remember, I was just thirteen. He had a great voice and I bought his album. I liked the Walker Brothers too and had their LP. In those days when you went to a gig you had the best of the bunch and I would have gone to see them all.

Jimi Hendrix was awesome. He was a man before his time.

The former ABC Cinema building in Aldershot which is facing demolition under redevelopment plans. (Author's collection)

Three
The Kinks and the Yardbirds On Tour

Girls, they've really got you now

THERE WAS EXCITEMENT for young music fans up and down the country at the end of April 1965 at the prospect of seeing two of the UK's mostly highly rated bands playing in their local High Street. The Kinks and the Yardbirds were setting off on a twenty-one-date tour that started off with all the usual screaming mayhem at the Slough Adelphi on 30 April.

To get two major bands on one show was a treat for those 1960s pop-pickers, but it was not a rare treat. In fact, it was typical of the 1960s pop package. Consider then that you not only got those two but also some up-and-coming Americans known as the Walker Brothers, and something really special for the fellas – an all-girl foursome from New York who went under the name of Goldie and the Gingerbreads. Never mind the Spice Girls, this was real girl power. Goldie and her mates could really rock – and they played their own instruments.

As if that little lot was not enough, on drums with one of the support bands, the Riot Squad, was a certain John 'Mitch' Mitchell, who was so good that he was later to hold down that job in the Jimi Hendrix Experience.

Mind you, not every town was lucky. Bolton, Leeds and Derby, the last three on the tour, missed out on both the Kinks and the Yardbirds for reasons that will become clear.

The Kinks, after a rocky beginning to their chart careers, were by this time riding the wave of popularity. Their first two singles had bombed and they were in danger of being dropped by their record company before they achieved their big breakthrough in August 1964 with *You Really Got Me*. The record got to number one and follow-up single *All Day And All Of The Night* did almost as well, reaching number two and

Goldie keeps her Gingerbreads in line with a bit of girl power. (Courtesy of Genya Ravan)

staying on the charts for fourteen weeks. The beginning of 1965 had seen them back at the very top with *Tired Of Waiting For You*.

As for the Yardbirds, this was the band that can boast of having Eric Clapton, Jimmy Page and Jeff Beck in its line-up over the years. But which of these three legends did the teenagers see on this 1965 tour? The answer is Jeff Beck. The Yardbirds had five Top Ten hits in 1965/66, but the band was never really a 'commercial' outfit. In fact, the commercialism of the first of those hits, *For Your Love*, tipped Clapton over the edge and he quit the band in March 1965 to join John Mayall's Bluesbreakers so he could remain close to his musical roots.

The spot was then offered to one of the industry's top young session men, Jimmy Page, but he was having enough fun and making enough money doing sessions. However, he recommended Jeff Beck, who accepted the job. Page finally joined the band a year later, initially on bass.

The unstable nature of the band's music and line-up reflected the struggle going on within it. At heart the Yardbirds were a hardened R&B outfit, but they needed chart success too.

Their first recordings were as a backing band for Chicago blues legend Sonny Boy Williamson, but they got noticed when they took over the Rolling Stones' residency at the Crawdaddy Club in Richmond in 1963. The Yardbirds were a class live act. Their 1964 live album, *Five Live Yardbirds*, featuring some classic Clapton riffs, said more about them than any of their singles.

As the tour got underway, *For Your Love* was slipping out of the Top Ten after spending weeks on the charts. That hit was enough to earn them the screams from the girls, while the guys would have appreciated their mature and classy R&B.

The *NME* announced two weeks before the start of the tour that the Yardbirds would have to miss four dates. The Rockin' Berries would replace them in Aldershot and they would also miss the last three nights.

On the opening night at Slough there was the predictable barrage of screams for the Kinks and the Yardbirds with the girls jumping up and down on the seats and waving their scarves. The mustard-suited Yardbirds, with Beck showing no sign of nerves, had a particularly hard job to be heard above the din the girls were making. What did cut through were some devastating licks from Beck and some searing vocals from singer Keith Relf.

The Yardbirds closed the first half with their set list for this tour: *Too Much Monkey Business, I Ain't Done Wrong, I Ain't Got You, Five Long Years, For Your Love* and *I'm A Man.*

The Kinks, who had the honour of closing the show, cranked up the screams. They made an explosive entrance. The stage was in darkness for the unmistakeable opening chords of *You Really Got Me.* On came the dazzling spotlight as the place went wild. They rocked on with *Beautiful Delilah, It's All Right, Tired Of Waiting For You, Everybody's Gonna Be Happy,* plus *All Day And All Of The Night,* before closing with *All Aboard.*

A report in that weekend's *Disc* said bassist Peter Quaife looked a little subdued, but Ray Davies was enjoying the spotlight. The paper described him bouncing around the stage, pulling off his jacket and 'looking for all the world like a mad magician'!

The fact that everyone was there to see the two star acts made it difficult for rest of the bill. Compère Bob Bain had a hard time keeping the attention of the audience, as did folk duo John and Jeff and sixteen-year-old female tour debutante Val McKenna in her white trouser suit, who had the misfortune to open the second half before the Kinks. Goldie and the Gingerbreads, in pale blue pyjama suits, gamely battled through their songs, *Can't You Hear My Heartbeat, I Can't Stand It* and *That's Why I Love You.*

The screaming continued as the tour swept on from Slough into Walthamstow, Lewisham and Portsmouth, and the headline acts were enjoying each other's company. The music papers reported on the Yardbirds' and the Kinks' increasing efforts to sabotage each other's performances with a series of practical jokes.

Beck said it started one night when the Kinks messed around with the mikes during *For Your Love.* Yardbird drummer Jim McCarty evened things up by strolling across the stage in an old hat and coat muttering to himself while the bemused Kinks were in full flight on stage. The Kinks stoked it up another notch at Lewisham when Dave Davies got his revenge on the Yardbirds' drummer by secretly removing the pin from his stool so that he crashed to the floor at the start of their opening number.

There were limits, however, even for pop stars, and the star bands happily thought better of a cunning plan to soak lesser lights John

Pam Newman, or Pam Newbury as she was in the 1960s. (Courtesy of Pam Newman)

Pam Newman with her grandson Josh. (Courtesy of Pam Newman)

We thought it would be great if we could tie the whole thing together and do sketches in between numbers and then have a finale with everyone coming on at the end and singing and jumping around.

This grand plan was a non-starter, but Quaife promised fans they would let rip and come up with some unexpected antics on stage to make the most of their short time in the spotlight.

The tour was rocking. Those opening night scenes of girls dancing on their seats and waving their scarves were repeated up and down the country as the Kinks and the Yardbirds strutted their stuff. The Kinks had to fork out for a new pair of wing mirrors on virtually a daily basis as overexcited fans took to stealing them for souvenirs.

The Yardbirds had negotiated Mondays off from the tour, but they just ended up facing other commitments. At least there were a lot of dates within a reasonable driving distance of London on this tour so the stars could get home if they wanted rather than having to bed down at some grimy B&B.

The Yardbirds were unavailable when the tour reached the ABC Cinema at Aldershot on Wednesday 5 May. However, the Aldershot public were more than happy to enjoy the Rockin' Berries and rising stars the Walker Brothers, plus Goldie and the girls, whose new record, *That's Why I Love You*, was out that week. The line-up was completed by the Riot Squad, the Mickey Finn, Jeff and Jon, and Val McCallum, plus compère Bob Bain who was still gamely trying to make himself heard.

Mick Redfern, who was in the audience that night, recalls the dramatic entrance of the Kinks:

They had a sort of extension to the stage at the front and when the Kinks came on they were in total darkness. Then you heard those famous chords and then the lights came on as they launched into *You Really Got Me*.

Everything was so loud – there was screaming thoughout.

Also there was his friend Mick Jordan of Haig Road, Aldershot. He said:

I've got six brothers and some of us went to that show. It was great because we had never had all the big groups here before. They would appear at Guildford and places like that, but they had never come to Aldershot.

I was into groups like the Rolling Stones, but I would have gone along for the whole thing really. The Kinks were good. They were wearing red jackets, I remember that and I recall the Walker Brothers playing too. I went to most of the ABC shows.

Also there was fifteen-year-old Pamela Newbury who was with a school friend from Cove Secondary Modern just a few miles down the road in Farnborough. Pam said:

I remember those red jackets the Kinks were wearing that night, and they had frilly shirts on too. They were pictured in those jackets on

and Jeff with a bucket of water while they were doing their big number – *Jailer Bring Me Water*.

The practical jokes lifted the spirits, but for the Kinks, at least, it was all papering over the cracks. They were already getting tired of the restrictions of the packaged pop tour. They wanted to give their fans more than just a 20-minute glimpse of what they could do.

Days before the tour, the boys were making television appearances in Paris, but Quaife took time out to tell the music press that they were planning more adventurous stage performances:

Ray (Davies) came up with the suggestion of having the whole thing turned into a proper show instead of just one act after another coming on, doing three or four numbers, and going off again, which is a bit of a drag.

The chaos and mayhem of the pop package gig.
(Aldershot News)

the front of one of their albums. I don't remember anything about the Walker Brothers or Goldie and the Gingerbreads – I was just there for the Kinks.

My dad had a car, so he probably dropped us off, and probably to the earlier show. I seem to remember that my mum got the tickets as a treat because she knew I loved the Kinks.

They were good that night, and I enjoyed it and I bet I was one of the girls screaming. That was the first concert I'd been to, so it was a bit special. We were upstairs. I can't be sure if it was that night, but I did manage to talk to Dave Davies, but it was very brief. I just said hello and then felt stupid, but I loved Ray and Dave, like you do when you're fifteen. We were all excited because you didn't expect someone like that to come to Aldershot.

As the excitement boiled over for the Kinks, there was an unhappy note for one unfortunate fourteen-year-old girl from Guildford. She was with a group of girls trying to attract the attention of the Kinks by kicking their dressing room window. The other girls scarpered when a policeman suddenly appeared from around the corner, just as the glass shattered! The girl was left to face the music alone, picking up a £1 fine, plus £1 costs, for 'willful damage of a window'.

The tour gave Goldie and the Gingerbreads an opportunity to spread their fan base. The star of the band was singer Goldie Zelkowitz. She was born in Poland in April 1945 and had been christened Genya but after the family moved to the United States, her mother began calling her Goldie because Genya sounded too un-American. She later reverted to Genya, adding the Ravan by the time the Gingerbreads disbanded in 1968. Guitarist Carol MacDonald, keyboard player Margo Crocitto and drummer Ginger Bianco completed the line-up.

The girls were New Yorkers who had made their debut at the Peppermint Lounge. Their big breakthrough came when Animals frontman Eric Burdon and manager Mike Jeffries heard them at the Wagon Wheel on 45th Street. Within a week they were to become the first all-female band to be signed to a major label, Atlantic, and they were soon on their way to England where they toured with the Rolling Stones and the Hollies. Beatle Ringo Starr and Rolling Stone Brian Jones were among the converts, as was Alan Price, who produced their first hit, *Can't You Hear My Heartbeat?*

After departing Aldershot, the show rolled into the Granada Cinema at Kingston-upon-Thames the next night, and then Unit Four Plus Two joined for the date at the Granada in East Ham, London, on 7 May.

The next night, Saturday 8 May, the show moved up to Stoke-on-Trent, at the Gaumont Cinema in Hanley. This was immediately followed by a private all-nighter at the Place in Hanley, featuring the Kinks, Goldie and the Gingerbreads, the Riot Squad and the Hipster Image. The Place was credited with launching several R&B names in the 1960s. On this night, the stars played for their own amusement – the beat starting at 12.45 a.m. and crashing on until 5.30 a.m. Ah, the energy of youth!

Goldie and the Gingerbreads were making the most of their time in the spotlight. Their faces were becoming well known at hip London venues like the Cromwellian, where they were among the regular late-night visitors and were not averse to jumping up and performing a couple of impromptu numbers.

The bands earned their money on this tour. Without a break after the Hanley all-nighter, the show rolled on to the Coventry Theatre. Then it was the Odeon Cinema, Swindon, the Odeon at Southend and the Granada cinemas at Bedford and Tooting, before reaching the Winter Gardens at Bournemouth on Saturday 15 May.

The screaming girls really excelled themselves in the first house that night, but some older fans must have grabbed the tickets for the later show, where respectful applause was the order of the night.

From there it was on to the Gaumont Cinema in Ipswich the next night, followed by the legendary Marquee in London on the Monday, then the Gaumont Cinema in Taunton, before reaching the Capitol Cinema in Cardiff on the Wednesday. That Cardiff date proved fateful for the Kinks. A spectacular on-stage set-to between Dave Davies and drummer Mick Avory ended with Davies needing hospital treatment, but more of that later.

That explosive incident spelt a premature end of the tour for the Kinks, while the Yardbirds enjoyed top billing for the next night's gig at the Wolverhampton Gaumont. The group reacted well to their promotion and their powerful set went down well with the locals. The crowds in the streets outside afterwards reportedly rivalled in numbers those who had paid homage to the Rolling Stones in their recent visit.

It was not such a good night for the Walker Brothers, who should have closed the first half. Unfortunately, their van broke down twice on the way and they arrived in time to take part in the second half.

The tour ended in chaotic fashion. The Yardbirds dipped out to head north for a mini tour in Scotland, so with the Kinks also out of action, the Walkers took over as the main act for the last three shows, starting at the Bolton Odeon on Friday 21 May. The Hollies were drafted in to support them at the Leeds Odeon the next night.

Goldie and the Gingerbreads joined the Kinks and the Yardbirds on the absent list for the finale at the Derby Gaumont on 23 May. They flew back to the States that day for a recording session.

Those last three shows gave the emerging Walkers a taste of the spotlight. The Leeds gig provided evidence of their inexperience as performers. They received a wild reception as they strolled out in their casual outfits. Scott immediately introduced *Pretty Girls Everywhere*, a song that had sunk almost without trace in America, and then followed up with *I'll Be Satisfied* and *Money*. There was a great response to their 15-minute set, but it was a no-frills performance – no bows, no encores and they didn't play their hit song *Love Her*. They were, however, already learning their trade and they soon discovered the art of getting the maximum screams from their admirers.

The Walkers, of course, were not real brothers. 'Nothing is real' certainly applied to the names of plenty of pop stars from the period.

The band, formed in Los Angeles in 1964, consisted of drummer Gary Leeds, bass player and budding heartthrob Scott Engel, and guitarist John Maus. Gary had already toured England with P.J. Proby, who had suggested the Walkers should blow out America and kick-start their careers in the UK. It was to prove a good decision. Their next single, *Make It Easy On Yourself*, rocketed to number one that summer. They followed that up with *My Ship Is Coming In*, which hit number three in December 1965, and another number one, *The Sun Ain't Gonna Shine Anymore*, in the spring of 1966. Scott by then had his own teen army of fans, and when they next returned to Aldershot in April 1967, they were the star act – ahead of Engelbert Humperdinck, Cat Stevens and Jimi Hendrix.

The group were never to enjoy the level of success and popularity in America that they did in Britain. Ironically, many Americans had them down as part of the Brit invasion.

The Riot Squad drummer 'Mitch' Mitchell, one of a group of session men who made up the band, was to return to Aldershot two years later as drummer with Hendrix. In between he was with Georgie Fame's Blue Flames.

Manager Larry Page had secured the Riot Squad their spot on the Kinks tour and they released seven singles over the next two years – but every one flopped. The Riot Squad were Bob Evans (saxophone), Mike Martin (bass) Ron Ryan (guitar) Mark Stevens (organ) and Graham Bonney (vocals), with Mitchell on drums.

East-end boys the Mickey Finn were another band to release a batch of records, however, chart success eluded them also. They released six singles on five labels, but all that talent failed to chalk up a hit. In the run-up to the tour they released *The Sporting Life* as a single but, sadly, it went the same way as the others. They were: Richard Brand (drums), Alan Marks (vocals), Mick Stannard (bass), Micky Waller (guitar) and 'Fluff' (organ).

Golden days for Goldie and the girls

In a 2005 interview with the author, Goldie – Genya Ravan – recalled the fun atmosphere of life on the road in the 1960s when love and peace were in the air – apart from the regular bust-ups, of course.

Genya witnessed one famous set-to between two of the Kinks:

Dave Davies and drummer Mick Avory got into it big time – they had a full blown fight on stage. To this day, I don't know what it was about, but Dave kicked Mick's drums over and Mick hit him over the head with a cymbal and Dave actually passed out. Ray was hysterical. He was crying and everything and saying 'What did you do to my brother?'

As far as Goldie and the Gingerbreads were concerned, we just wanted to make sure the tour continued. We tried to dismiss it, telling reporters it was all part of the act. You know, *You Really Got Me*. But the truth was it was a big thing. The curtains had to close.

Avory stormed off that night in Cardiff while Dave Davies went to hospital. The band missed the last few dates of the tour and things were never to be quite the same for the Kinks. They patched things up, but it was evidence of the pressure pop stars were under in those days – particularly in the middle of arduous tours. This particular tour cost the Kinks two road managers, Brian Longstaff and Ray Dovedave, who announced they were quitting. Dovedave was quoted: 'I couldn't stand working with the boys any more. The tension was too much.'

Writing and recording, nightly gigs, television and radio dates, even longer and more demanding foreign tours. It was possible to go years with barely a day off and with mostly only each other for company. In those situations, teen idols who were little more than teenagers themselves settled for making their own entertainment. Goldie and the girls were not about to miss out on the fun. Genya said:

We would get thrown out of hotels sometimes. Us girls would have pillow fights or water fights ... or I would be caught in someone's room!

Me and Peter Quaife from the Kinks were sort of an item for a while and also me and Mick Jagger when we toured with the Rolling Stones. You've got to remember, that was our social life. That's how it was. We didn't have the chance to meet other guys and we were there with these people all the time when we were touring.

I had an enormous crush on Paul Jones from Manfred Mann. I thought he was fantastic – and also as a performer too. We toured with him when he was with Manfred Mann and also when he was solo and he was quite something.

When we toured with all the guys, we were like family. We were young and it was exciting. We would be practising our harmonies on the bus and the guys would join in, and they would run through their own stuff too, and we had great fun.

So what was it like being women in a business dominated by men? According to Genya:

It was a very rare thing to have an all-girl band that played their own instruments in those days, and Goldie and the Gingerbreads copped some flak.

People thought you were a freak. Some people said we were a lesbian band and others said we were too loose with the guys. You couldn't win.

Despite all that, Genya and the girls never regretted the decision to leave their native New York to seek fame and fortune in the UK. They

Genya Ravan, aka Goldie, still looking fab in late 2006. (Courtesy of Genya Ravan)

were first spotted by Animals frontman Eric Burdon and his manager Mike Jeffries in 1964 playing New York's Wagon Wheel on 45th Street. They were quickly signed to a major label and left for England. Soon after they arrived, they had a very important person banging the drum for them – Ringo Starr. Genya recalled:

Ringo was responsible for our first television appearance in England. He saw us jumping up and down doing our thing at the Flamingo, where so many people used to jam, and he thought we were the greatest thing since sliced bread. He met Peter Cook and Dudley Moore soon after and said to them You want to get an all-girl group on your show – and I know just the group.

Ringo was also responsible for turning us on to Indian food, and I didn't immediately thank him for the experience. It was so hot, I nearly killed him! Ringo and Harry Nilsson had taken us for that Indian meal and it was just before Ringo had his tonsils out, so he was very nervous.

Genya was never without her trusty record player on tour. It helped to pass the time when they weren't on stage. 'It went everywhere with me,' said Genya. 'I would never go on stage without a burst of Ray Charles first.' Genya also claims the credit for turning Yardbird Jeff Beck on to the music of blues legend Buddy Guy.

Goldie and the girls, like the other performers, got used to running the gauntlet of over-excited teenagers:

We loved the fans and remember the whole thing with such affection, but the truth is the fans scared the hell out of us at times. As soon as the bus pulled up we would be besieged by teenagers trying to get a piece of us. It could be pretty scary when you got a mob like that. I remember Brian Jones from the Rolling Stones, God rest his soul, in tears one time. They pulled a lock of his hair out – almost lifted his scalp – and he was crying. That's what it could be like – scary stuff. They would all get so excited.

Goldie recalls that Riot Squad drummer Mitch Mitchell was impressed by Goldie and the Gingerbreads, and so were the Stones. 'We were doing the Harlem Shuffle during those tours and then the Rolling Stones went and done it all those years later, the little bastards,' giggled Genya.

Touring with the likes of the Stones, Kinks and Yardbirds may have been an amazing experience, but Goldie and the girls weren't earning big bucks. 'We were on a strict salary of 100 dollars a week each, but at least they did pay our expenses. The money didn't go far – it was hardly enough. We had expenses in America to keep up and I wanted to send money home to my mother because I was still living at home.'

As the only females on tour, the girls were grateful for a protective arm around them from their star colleagues – but it was not enough to spare them the traditional final-night mayhem:

The Rolling Stones' favourite trick was to put their heads round the curtain while we were on stage, and of course there would suddenly be an almighty scream and we were shocked and thinking did someone drop their trousers or something?

But the Hollies were the wildest. On the last night of our tour with them they came out on to the stage while we were playing and they were wearing our wigs. We plotted our revenge. We tied a string round their drummer's stool and were going to pull it from under him, but, unfortunately, he spotted it.

Music aside, Genya had another talent:

I would cut the guys' hair for them. I did our girls too. Everyone liked my hair style and I was pretty handy with the scissors. Mine was called a shag haircut – it had an altogether more innocent meaning back then!

We were like family on the tours and our group was the best family of all. We rarely had an argument, but when we did, it was over the second we got playing. And we are still close to this day.

Four
The Hollies and the Small Faces

This town ain't big enough for the both of us!

THERE WAS SOME unexpected drama when the Aldershot ABC Cinema hosted the opening night of the Hollies' UK tour on 15 October 1966.

Fellow chart stars the Small Faces walked out just minutes before they were due to close the first half of the early evening show in a row over who should get top billing. The East End boys, fresh from claiming their first number one the previous month with *All Or Nothing*, clearly felt this should entitle them to close the show, but the Hollies were having none of it.

Tony Brooks, the cinema's chief projectionist, was working in the wings when the row erupted:

I remember hearing this kerfuffle and these raised voices. I didn't even bother to turn around. This was happening while one of the other acts was performing and I just had my mind set on doing my job. I wasn't going to be distracted.

Afterwards, I heard some of them talking about not going on. Again, I didn't get involved. My attitude was I'm here to do my job – sort it out yourselves!

Sadly, it could not be sorted out. The Small Faces insisted they were walking out unless they could close the show. ABC executive Joe Seal and co-tour promoter Peter Walsh desperately tried to persuade the group's manager Don Arden to get the boys to reconsider, but they were adamant. So out they walked, leaving their Aldershot fans heartbroken.

Compère Ray Cameron had to make the embarrassing announcement: 'Due to circumstances beyond our control, the Small Faces will be unable to appear here tonight.'

Paul Jones was sporting a particularly flowery shirt for this picture with his touring buddies, the Hollies. (Courtesy of Bobby Elliott)

Luckily, there was still plenty for the teenagers to get excited about, with the Hollies putting on a storming show, ably supported by special guest Paul Jones – on his first solo tour after leaving Manfred Mann – plus Paul and Barry Ryan, but there was still hostility in the air afterwards when the Hollies queued up to take a pop at their rivals for pulling out.

Asked if it was right that the Hollies should top the bill, frontman Allan Clarke snapped, 'There's no doubt about it.' Group leader Graham Nash, later to achieve even more acclaim in Crosby, Stills, Nash and Young, added cuttingly, 'It just shows how unprofessional some groups can be.' Lead guitarist Tony Hicks added, 'They ought to be renamed the Jokers.'

The fall out made the front pages of the national music press, with the Small Faces eventually making an embarrassing climb down – but only after also missing their hometown gig the next night. Singer Steve Marriott added ruefully, 'We were naturally sorry to have disappointed our fans, especially in our home area at Romford.'

Their agent Tito Burns claimed, 'It was a complete misunderstanding that has now been straightened out and the boys will be rejoining the tour.'

At least the Romford fans had the consolation of having a late replacement act – the New Vaudeville Band, whose current single *Winchester Cathedral* had raced up to number four in the Hit Parade, where it was to remain for another three weeks.

The Small Faces were back on board for the visit to the Cheltenham Odeon on the Tuesday. They did not let anyone down this time. Their monster hits *Whatcha Gonna Do About It?*, *Sha-La-La-La-Lee* and *All*

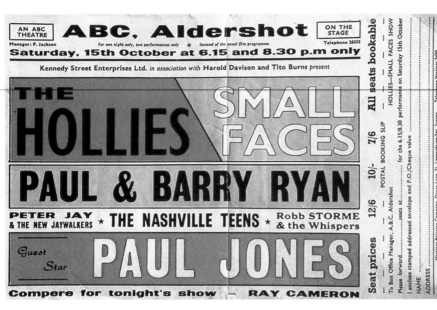

(*Left*) The Small Faces may have appeared on the handbill, but they did not appear on stage at the Aldershot ABC on the opening night of that 1966 Hollies tour. The handbill was another rescued by cinema staff.

(*Right*) Hollies fans captured by the *Aldershot News* at that 1966 concert.

Or Nothing were all in the set. However, the atmosphere between the two main bands on the nineteen-date three-week tour remained frosty.

The Aldershot opener began with Robb Storme and the Whispers who produced a lively little set, including *California Girls* and an unusual version of the theme tune from the television series *Batman*. The storm, however, was about to break.

The Nashville Teens got the party started, with Ray Phillips reportedly gyrating around the stage in a frenzied manner during their four numbers. At least compère Ray Cameron was able to make a happier announcement: 'They told me Aldershot was quiet. Boy, were they wrong. We've got a right bunch of ravers here!'

Then it was time for the screaming to start as identical twin brothers Paul and Barry Ryan, the sons of 1950s singer Marion Ryan, pitched into action, with the Whispers providing the backing. The Ryan brothers, who hailed from Leeds, had been signed to Decca the previous year, notching up several Top Twenty hits. They were proudly sporting their latest look – matching white Edwardian frock-coats, hipsters and boots – the outfits a snip at £30 a piece.

The teen heartthrobs took their lives in their hands by being the first stars to walk along the specially created walk-way into the screaming girls. In seconds flat the first girl – wearing a trouser suit – lunged at the boys and grabbed one in what was a very passable wrestling stranglehold. Step forward a bouncer to the rescue.

The Ryan boys were used to this kind of hysteria and effortlessly strolled through their set, featuring *What Now My Love? Don't Bring Me Your Heartaches, I Love Her, See See Rider* and *Have You Ever Loved Somebody?* During the latter number another girl braved the wrath of the bouncers to express her undying love at close quarters. The Ryans

were joined by their personal piper – their Scottish road manager Don Finlayson – complete in full Highland dress – for their final number, *I Love How You Love Me*. After the show Barry claimed that one of the fans who grabbed him on stage was a boy. Thank goodness for the interval so it could all calm down a bit.

As is often the case, rumours began to spread. The Hollies had not arrived in their dressing room but had been seen somewhere in the town, the story went. However, with a roll of drums the second half was underway with the five-member Peter Jay and the Jaywalkers. After their short set, compère Cameron was back in the spotlight to stoke the flames (if it were really necessary) for the appearance of special guest Paul Jones.

This was his first solo tour without his Manfred Mann buddies and he confessed to nerves before the show when he spoke to reporters in his dressing room, but nerves were not apparent when he strolled on stage to a barrage of teenage screams.

Backed by the Jaywalkers, he launched into his first number, appropriately entitled *Along Came Jones*. The screams grew yet louder as he followed up with *Pretty Flamingo*, a number one smash for Manfred Mann earlier that year. Then it was the tonsil-busting *Bony Moronie*, a hit for rock 'n' roll legend Larry Williams. Then he sang *Lady Godiva*, which at that moment was climbing the charts for Peter and Gordon. There was still time for two more numbers – his own current record *High Time* and finally *My Way*, not the Sinatra classic, but a ballad that Jones had chosen.

As he left the stage it was time for the protectors – made up of Securicor and St John Ambulance volunteers – to do their stuff again. They created a human barrier in front of the stage. Then the lights dimmed and after a pause beamed brightly again as the Hollies launched into *I Can't Let Go* which had spent ten weeks in the charts, rising to number two, earlier that year.

Tearful teens, screaming for all they were worth, gathered up their energies for another determined series of assaults on the stage, but the human wall held strong. Undaunted, the bill-toppers carried on with Graham Nash discarding his guitar to join singer Allan Clarke for *You Don't Know Like I Know*, climaxing with a solo from drummer Bobby Elliott. The drummer pulled out all the stops, gashing his finger on a splintered drumstick as he pounded away.

Still the hits rolled on. The classic *A Taste Of Honey*, Bob Dylan's *The Times They Are A-Changin'* and their summer smash *Bus Stop*, which had been in the charts for nine weeks. Then followed their current release *Stop Stop Stop*, which eventually peaked at number two, and a cover version of the Four Tops' current smash *Reach Out And I'll Be There*.

The screams went into overdrive and the Hollies somehow made it back to their dressing room for a champagne celebration at the end of the first show. Then, after a short break to catch their breath, everything started from scratch again for the second house at 8.30 p.m!

The night that had started amid such controversy ended in triumph for the Hollies. In the audience at Aldershot that night to witness the start of the tour were Graham Nash's wife Rosemary and her sister Anne. Allan Clarke's wife Jenny and Tony Hicks' girlfriend, the model Jane Lumb, were also there, as was Barry Ryan's girlfriend, Samantha Juste.

The Hollies had only been back from America one day before the gig, but Graham Nash said the Aldershot atmosphere was special. He said later:

Our reception on the first night was tremendous – the Americans weren't as wild as that, except when we played with the Beach Boys before about 15,000 kids.

At Aldershot I was dragged offstage once and I was amazed at the strength of one girl who got hold of me. It took four bouncers to drag her off.

We couldn't hear any of what we were playing because of the screaming, so I hope it sounded all right.

Paul Jones was also excited about his Aldershot reception. In a music column that week, he wrote:

So my first show as a solo singer is over – and what a relief that is! I was so nervous and tense wondering how the audience would react.

And it didn't help when the Small Faces pulled out and someone asked if I'd take their place by closing the first half. Then they decided they didn't want me to, after all. It was a drag, losing the Faces for the first night, but the show was saved by a very good tour manager, plus Paul and Barry and the Hollies being so very good.

I sang *Pretty Flamingo* because although it associates me with my old group, it is so me, don't you think?

Robb Storme and the Whispers. (Courtesy of Eddie McManus)

I wondered how a hit from the rocking fifties like *Bony Moronie* would go down and was very pleased with its reception. It was always a great favourite of mine – shows how old I am! I recorded *Lady Godiva* four months ago – before Peter and Gordon's version. It will be on my first LP, which comes out in early December.

(*Left*) **Bobby Elliott pictured in his pre-Hollies days of 1963.** (Courtesy of Bobby Elliott)

(*Right*) **Bobby Elliott pictured in 2006 by Rob Haywood.** (Courtesy of Bobby Elliott)

These concerts were not just about screaming girls. The lads were also happy to be seen at the shows – particularly smart young mods like Bryan Green of North Lane, Aldershot, who attended several of the ABC pop shows and was there for that opening night:

Paul and Barry Ryan were very smart in their gear – I remember their white outfits. They were good looking lads and the girls were going mad – there was so much screaming. I'm fairly sure I bunked in for the show and was standing over to one side near the wall. There were a few empty seats as the girls were gathering around the stage. As I was standing there Tony Hicks from the Hollies winked over at me and I felt like I was the bee's knees – innocent fun.

On hand to witness events for the *Aldershot News* that night at the ABC was young reporter Richard Holiday who was to embark on his own successful Fleet Street career. Richard recalls being in the dressing room before the show. He caught the full blast as Small Faces manager Don Arden, with his stars in mutiny, stormed around. Richard recalls:

I was chatting to Paul Jones. What a charming man he was, and I have no doubt still is. Then all of a sudden this fella burst in shouting and swearing. He pointed at me and said who the xxxxxxx hell is he? Paul said 'It's OK, he's with the local paper.' 'Well tell him he can xxxx off' came the reply. With that he was gone. I asked Paul who he was. He's Don Arden, he said. Don't mind him. He's well known in the business. Everyone knows what he's like.

Looking back all these years later, it might surprise some to know that Arden, the man who came out with all that language, is Sharon Osbourne's father!

Incidentally, The Hollies weren't averse to walking out. Even before the tour had finished they stormed off TV's *Ready Steady Go* because the Dave Clark Five were given the spot above them and the Londoners had not had a hit for nearly a year!

I'll smash your Small Face in!

Hollies drummer Bobby Elliott was a stunned spectator as blows were traded in the row between his group and the Small Faces on that fateful opening night.

In the blue corner was the Hollies' tour manager Rod Shields, sticking to his guns that his boys were topping the bill, and in the red with rage corner, the Small Faces manager Don Arden, who was determined that his lads would close the show. 'He was trying to bully us really, and there was no way we were having that,' Bobby recalled. 'It didn't amount to a full-on brawl, but Don Arden pushed Rod quite hard in the chest and Rod responded by smacking him equally hard across the face. A lot of words were exchanged.

'They tried to pull one over on us, basically. They thought we would capitulate, and we weren't falling for it.'

Relations remained frosty after the Small Faces rejoined the tour.

'I used to hang around with them. As far as I was concerned, it (the trouble) was over,' said Bobby, 'but I don't think Graham Nash or the others felt the same way. They really didn't want anything to do with them after that.'

Even the powerful publicity machine failed to prevent negative headlines in the national music press. The constant jostling for billing was the problem. Paul and Barry Ryan squeezed themselves ahead of the Faces for one gig, before the London boys flexed their muscles to win their spot back.

The frostiness between the bands was lost on their fans who were having a whale of a time. They almost overturned Paul Jones' car outside the Odeon at Cheltenham on the tour's third gig. The Small Faces' Jag window was a casualty of the mayhem as the tour departed Cheltenham for the Capitol Cardiff the next night.

However, the tension was creating casualties. Hollie Allan Clarke, feeling run down, had a medical check-up when the tour reached Cardiff. Steve Marriott was quoted: 'I haven't enjoyed this tour as much as others because of the bickering. The only time I like it is when I'm playing. Otherwise, I feel as if I could cut the atmosphere with a knife. It's an overall general feeling. No one raves about with anyone. Everyone sticks to their own little scene.'

Nashville Teen Ray Phillips picked up the bad vibes. 'I've never been on a tour like it,' he said. 'On all the others, the groups mixed with each other backstage. Maybe it would be different if everyone travelled together, but the Hollies, Faces and Paul Jones have their own cars.'

Peter Jay, by then a veteran of the touring scene, said: 'Everyone seems to be taking things too seriously. They're all conscious of trying to go down the best and it's interfering with the social side.'

Steve Marriott, Ian 'Mac' McLagan, Kenney Jones and Ronnie 'Plonk' Lane proved that the Small Faces could do stylish on tour. (*Aldershot News*)

Pity the poor tour manager Fred Perry who had the job of juggling all those egos. He described it as the most troublesome of forty-six tours he had been on all over the world.

It wasn't all bad news, however. Despite the in-fighting, the music was great and the fans were loving it. Four major acts vying for the limelight meant a top-quality money-spinning show. There were full houses up and down the country and all the mayhem that went with it.

As the tour left Cardiff and reached Taunton to play the Gaumont the next night, compère Ray Cameron had to work so hard to get over the screams that he lost his voice. At least Ray's misfortune meant a bit of peace and quiet later on for Nash, who even at that late hour was busy bashing out the lyrics of a new song on the hotel's old typewriter!

The tension between the bands was nothing compared with the anger of jealous boyfriends, as Small Faces star Steve Marriott recorded with commendable humour in that weekend's *Disc and Music Echo*:

At some shows there have been girls rushing the stage almost every five seconds. They grab me and knock me out of tune, but I don't mind – they're there to have a ball, so great.

Some of the boys aren't so friendly, though. Some geezers tried to have a go at us after the Taunton show. But I think I would get the needle if a girlfriend of mine was screaming at a group. I'd knock her out first, then the geezer!

There was no let-up. The bands were on good form in Wolverhampton the next night, where they could be heard despite the screaming and the fifteen girls who got themselves into such a state that they needed treatment from St John Ambulance Brigade workers.

The Hollies' latest hit, *Stop Stop Stop*, was a high spot and their version *of Reach Out And I'll Be There* brought a tumultuous finale for them. The Small Faces and the Ryan twins also worked the girls into a frenzy, despite the curtains closing on the Ryans in the middle of a song in one of the houses. Paul Jones launched into *Pretty Flamingo* and Peter Jay and the Jaywalkers, with their new sixteen-year-old singer Terry Reid, also caught the ear.

The next three nights saw gigs at the ABC Cinema, Peterborough, the ABC at Hull and the Gaumont at Ipswich before everyone could finally take a breather with a day off on Tuesday 25 October.

The tour then resumed with gusto with successive gigs at the ABC Northampton, the Cambridge Regal, the Lincoln ABC, the Chester ABC and the Coventry Theatre. The final week commenced with a trip to the Worcester Gaumont on Tuesday 1 November, and the final four gigs, on successive nights from Thursday 3 November, were at the Odeon Manchester, the Odeon at Leeds and the City Hall, Sheffield, with Newcastle having the pleasure of hosting the tour's finale at the City Hall.

Touring was always relentless and this one had never really recovered from the unpleasantness of that opening night, but it would be wrong to give the impression that it was all tension, jealousy and bickering. Friendships were made on most tours.

Looking back in 2005, Bobby Elliott said the Kinks drummer Mick Avory, and Tony Jackson's drummer Paul Francis, were two of his big pals.

Then there was the tour with the Rolling Stones. Bobby said:

We knew them quite well. Charlie (Watts) was very laid back – easy going, but straight talking. He said it how it was. We worked with the Beatles too.

It was fun in the early days, mixing with all the other musicians on the tour bus. It was right for the time, a coming together. We were young guys starting out in the business and it was great, being able to chat with everyone.

But of course, as time went on and back catalogues grew and acts were developed we all wanted more time to show what we could do.

Make sure you spell our names right... Steve Marriott, Ian 'Mac' McLagan, Kenney Jones and Ronnie 'Plonk' Lane impart words of wisdom to reporter Steve Mann.
(*Aldershot News*)

Were the Sixties as great for the stars as they were for the fans, though? According to Elliott:

I wouldn't change a thing. Everyone seems to talk it up, but when I sit down and think about it – which I don't often do – it was great.

There are so many memories. There was Jimi Hendrix's opening night at the Bag O' Nails when I was sitting in the front row with Bill Wyman, and the night in another club with Jimmy Page when he was talking about putting this band together that ended up being Led Zeppelin!

Oh, and one other Hollies set-to, this time in print, has been happily resolved. Unpleasantries were exchanged when Beatle George Harrison was quoted rubbishing the Hollies version of his song *If I Needed Someone* in December 1965. All these years later, Elliott says he has discovered that George had not made the comment – it had come from someone at the Beatles press office who had taken it upon themselves to stir it up. 'The truth finally came out at a dinner party with George's son Dhani,' he said.

Along Came Jones, the new solo star

Special guest Paul Jones was not on hand to witness the backstage bust-up between Rod Shields and Don Arden as the Small Faces stormed out of that Hollies show in 1966. The overpowering memory for the Manfreds singer, looking back in May 2005, was the sheer talent of the East End boys:

I toured Australia and New Zealand with the Small Faces and they were a brilliant group – absolutely tremendous. When they went on stage they just gave everything. I've seen Stevie Marriott hyperventilate with the effort he was putting into a vocal. He had this fantastic voice – unique and quite influential. A lot of people have tried to sound like that and as for the rest of them what musicians – fantastic. They were just top notch, number one – premier division. I'm not interested in what they may have messed up – I'm interested in what they could do, and they could do it supremely well.

Jones was also an admirer of the Hollies:

I remember chatting with the Hollies in their dressing room a few times. I got on very well with them, especially Tony (Hicks). He was just one of those very likeable people. In fact, I found them all pleasant and likeable, but Tony was particularly gregarious. He was the one who spent more time mixing with everybody else – him and Bobby (Elliott). Great band too.

Looking back at the press coverage from the opening night, Jones remarked:

So this is obviously the news story, the fact that the Faces weren't there. You can see how big rhythm and blues was in those days – even Paul and Barry Ryan had to do some! I think the song *My Way* that I did, not the Sinatra one of course, came from a Broadway musical, although I must admit to having copied my version from the Marvin Gaye recording.

What's interesting is that I did that show, apparently performing six songs, which isn't much, is it? Also, I didn't do *Do Wah Diddy* and *If You Gotta Go, Go Now*, which were big records for me. Of course, I could have done *5-4-3-2-1* which was another. I suppose I was trying not to do too many Manfred songs.

By the time of that 1966 show, Jones had left the touring bus behind and was being chauffeur driven to gigs in his own Rolls-Royce. He had served his time with Manfred Mann and wasn't at all daunted to be facing the future as a solo artist:

I'd spent three and a half years with the Manfreds – two and a half years of it pretty much at the top. And so I guess I was fairly confident at the time. I left the group and went straight on to do a movie – Privilege – with Peter Watkins. It wasn't mentioned in the review so it probably hadn't come out yet, but the filming must have been July/August/September so I had probably not long finished the filming and here I was being driven in a Rolls-Royce, with my own road manager. I didn't sit in the back, I sat alongside the driver, but you know, money and hit records and stuff tends to give you a reasonable amount of confidence.

I must have had a bit too much confidence, because to go out there on my first tour after leaving the Manfreds and not do *Do Wah Diddy* strikes me as being rash and perhaps self-centered – perhaps a bit vain, a bit big headed. You know, 'I don't need to do *Do Wah Diddy*, I'm a big star'.

I might have suffered from a bit of that in the second half of the 1960s, but nowadays I don't worry about doing that stuff. I wonder whether I ever said that *Pretty Flamingo* was so me?

Paul can still recall his first touring experience when Manfred Mann shared the bus with Joe Brown and the Bruvvers, the Crystals and Johnny Kidd and the Pirates. 'There was also a young solo singer called Kevin Kirk who was more of a throwback to the rock 'n' roll time, because this was a bit later, at the very beginning of 1964 just when *5-4-3-2-1* came in the charts.'

Paul Jones, as pictured in the *Aldershot News*, signing an autograph for Philippa Bradford before the show in October 1966.

The Manfreds had an added responsibility on that tour. They had to accompany any artist who hadn't got a band – and that became awkward after *5-4-3-2-1* became a hit. 'Suddenly, we were stars. We didn't argue about where we were on the bill, but we did get out of accompanying all these unknown people, which would have seemed a bit strange for them, anyway.'

There was one exception – The Crystals. 'We agreed to go on backing them because we'd done the rehearsals and we knew how to do the stuff. We'd be standing there behind them, dutifully doing our best, but come on, we were kids, and if the girls screamed for us we didn't pretend we weren't enjoying it. And that used to be hard for the girls some nights. But nonetheless, that was our job because we said we would do it.'

Of course, being the centre of attention on stage had its attractions. 'We didn't have a hit until 1964, by which time I was nearly twenty-two. I should have been a little bit more responsible than I turned

out to be, but come on, twenty-one to twenty-two, you're mad aren't you really? You do the music because you love the music, but as soon as that other stuff happens – wahey!'

It wasn't all screams and adulation. Being on stage in the 1960s held its dangers:

There were moments back then that I hated. There was a gig I remember in South Wales. People think that thing about people throwing beer bottles at the band started with punk. We had it in the 1960s. All it wanted was for some seventeen year old's girlfriend to be screaming at the band and he'd throw a beer bottle at us. He'd love to break somebody's nose, or cut their mouth or something. That happened a couple of nights, but not many. Most of the time it was terrific fun.

Paul's voice has retained its power and quality after more than forty years in the business, but it was put under considerable strain by the poor sound systems on those early tours:

I used to have the most dreadful problems with my voice because I was always shouting and screaming to hear myself. It was ghastly. There were no foldback monitors, so you didn't hear your voice coming back. At the same time, the amps they were using behind you were not

anything like as powerful as nowadays. Little Vox AC30s and things like that. The music wasn't drowning you so much, it was more the girls actually.

In fact, there is a story which I remember very distinctly. We were playing somewhere on the east coast and we got back to the dressing room after a particularly average gig from the musical point of view, but total success from the audience point of view. This was quite late on – 1966 – we had probably just had *If You Gotta Go, Go Now* hit number two, and *Pretty Flamingo*, hit number one. We came back to the dressing room and I kind of flopped down in the chair and our tenor saxophone player at the time, a very fine musician called Len Dobson, announced that he was leaving the band. And there was a kind of stunned silence and Manfred said 'Why Len?' And Len said 'Before the gig started, when I opened my saxophone case, I took out my saxophone and put the mouthpiece on and then I looked for a reed, and I hadn't got any. Not even one. I have just been on stage with you guys miming my way through the gig, and not only did the audience not notice, none of you even noticed'. And he said 'That's not music to me, and that's why I'm going'.

Jones had already been planning his own exit from the band:

I gave my notice in September 1965 and it was nearly July 1966 when I left, so I guess I wasn't wholly taking it all seriously anyway – as my manager was negotiating a new record deal for me!

It was kind of crazy, all that screaming stuff, and also of course, with those package tours you had this strange situation where you only had six songs. You were big if you had 30 minutes.

Peter Jay's Jaywalkers backed Jones on that first solo venture, and Paul retains fond memories:

I remember touring with them. I was reminded of that time when I was up in the Fens only the other day with the Manfreds. There was this sign to Fosdyke and I remember that I called Peter Jay's guitarist the Fosdyke kid. Whether he came exactly from Fosdyke or from somewhere round about there I don't know, but I'm talking about Terry Reid, who later went on to do a single called *The Hand Don't Fit The Glove*.

And gosh, he should be a major star to this day, because I'll tell you something, I had a hard time with that kid. It may not have been on this tour, it might have been slightly later, but whenever we got anywhere near where Terry was at all well known there was a clack of girls who used to scream for him when I was on stage and he was behind me playing accompaniment.

It's scream time again for the girls at the front.
(*Aldershot News*)

The pub lock-in that saved the Teens from the teenies

Let's get one thing clear from the start. They may be called the Nashville Teens, but the band actually hailed from Weybridge in Surrey, and by the time they joined that 1966 Hollies/Small Faces tour, they were already chart veterans.

Tobacco Road had been a smash hit in the summer of 1964, and they followed that up with *Google Eye*, which also hit the Top Ten that year. The next three singles failed to hit those dizzy heights, but the Teens – Art Sharp and Ray Phillips (vocals), Peter Harris (bass), John Allen (guitar), Barry Jenkins (drums) and John Hawken (piano) – were respected as a gritty live band.

Like so many top Brit bands, they had earned their lumps and learned their trade in the tough Reeperbahn district of Hamburg and since then they had toured Britain with rock 'n' roll legends Jerry Lee Lewis, Chuck Berry and Carl Perkins, along with many other household names.

When they arrived in Aldershot for the ABC gig in October 1966, they did what all good rock stars do – they hit the pub.

Fan Martyn Wright, a friend of Art Sharp's for more than forty years, was in the Pegasus before and after the show and recalls a rather unusual lock-in. He said:

After the show, the bands headed over the road to the pub. The Hollies were there, so was Peter Jay and the guy who played bagpipes for Paul and Barry Ryan. Peter Noone was there too. He wasn't on that tour, but he just came along to see the bands I suppose. There were probably others there too.

I was having a chat with Peter Noone. It had been in the press that day that he had just signed a film contract worth a million dollars. He said if he was getting a million, then Mickie Most (Noone's producer) must have been getting two or three million. He said he didn't mind, as he was getting paid so much.

At that point Art came over and said if you're doing that well, you can get the drinks in for the boys – and fair play to him, he did.

By this time the word had got out that everyone was in the pub and the kids were swarming around outside. The landlord had to lock us in before it got out of hand. The police came over in the end and said we all had to leave.

These days top stars are not shy of making the most outlandish demands; dressing rooms must be stocked with all sorts of weird and wonderful goodies. Teens Art Sharp and Peter Harris can testify that the 1960s touring scene was very different. Sharp said:

I slept right through the Small Faces rehearsal at Gloucester – that's how knackered I was. There was no food or drink in the dressing room. After sleeping on the bus we'd arrive at the next venue, clean our teeth and have a shave, and that was it.

I also remember turning up at this bed and breakfast in Leicester with Ray (Phillips). We knocked on the door several times – no reply. So Ray and I eventually pushed the door open and we heard this strange voice calling out. We went into this room and there was a woman of about 100 in the bed and I think she was paralysed. She sent Ray to get some water. With all the strength she could muster, she said 'These are your terms. Room 10s 6d. Room with hot water 12s 6d. Hot water was a rare luxury in those days. Anyway, we went back after the gig and what a place! John thought it was haunted and jammed a chair against the door and we discovered that the two bob extra for hot water was the kettle!

Another B&B at Elgin in Scotland proved just as spartan. Bassist Peter Harris recalled:

All the homes in Elgin seemed to be made of granite – they were like tombstones, very grim.

This particular place was 12s 6d with the hot water and the landlady was probably the Scottish equivalent of a Methodist. She said: 'You'll be having breakfast.' Yes. 'You'll be having porridge.' It wasn't a question! 'You'll be taking milk in your porridge. You'll be taking salt in your porridge.' And high tea was bacon and eggs – it was like breakfast.

Sharp added: 'A grand life – I couldn't do it again!'

Even such humble bed and breakfast accommodation was a rare treat for the Teens on tour:

We usually slept on the tour bus. That's how it was. It was a rare luxury to get a B&B. If we did, it was usually over a pub, or something like that. At one place the landlady said the bed had heat in. Usually, the beds were so cold and damp, you went to bed fully clothed! Everything was damp in the 1960s. Anyway, there was a piece of wire leading from the bed and a plug and then I realised what the 'heat' was – it was a car mechanic's light bulb. Luxury. That was where your bum went – the head and feet got cold.

Travelling could be tricky too. Harris said:

We played a gig near Sunningdale. We were playing at a local hall, but there was a thick fog, as there often seemed to be in those days. My bass speakers were huge so we had to use Art's van. But the fog was so thick that we couldn't see anything so I had to sit on the front bonnet to guide the driver. It couldn't happen today.

We had bought this old Daimler ambulance. We went to Cologne in that. It was great – such a comfortable ride. There's still some of them around. But if we'd got a puncture we would have had it – luckily, we never did. Customs stopped us at Dover once and ripped it apart. It was also searched by police in New Haw once when they were looking for the Great Train Robbers. Apparently, they were following up a rumour that the loot was stashed there.

Of course, there were the usual antics. Harris recalled:

Fatch, one of our roadies, got caught smoking pot at Swadlingcote. The local bobby had come along to see we were alright and Fatch was in the corner smoking a joint. He threw his arms up and said Okay, it's a fair cop. The bobby didn't know what he was talking about because he was only the local beat bobby and had probably never smelt a joint. But as soon as he was alerted by Fatch, he felt he had to do something about it, so poor Fatch got arrested.

Then there was the tour with Chuck Berry and Carl Perkins. Sharp said, 'Chuck Berry ended up at the back of the bus when we were on tour with him. Carl Perkins said, Where I come from boy, blacks go to the back of the coach. Chuck loved it though, because it meant he could have two seats and he was able to have his way with a young girl singer!'

He also recalled a horse ride with a Hollie. 'After we played in Manchester one night I slept on Allan Clarke's sofa. He lived just outside Manchester. LA he called it – that's Lower Altrincham. Anyway, he said we're going horse riding. I'd never been on a horse. It did what it wanted to do. As soon as they opened the gate it went off like a rocket. I literally had my arms around its throat.'

The band headed for New York as part of Murray the K's Christmas Show in 1964. Also on the bill were singer Chuck Jackson, Ben E. King, the Drifters, the Shirelles and the Shangri-Las, plus the Zombies and an up and coming nineteen-year-old starlet called Dionne Warwick.

There was an added bonus for motorbike fan Harris who got to ride one on stage to rev up for the intro of *Leader Of The Pack* by The Shangri-Las.

The band was getting a frenzied reception from the New York teens – much to the discomfort of bassist Harris. 'I had the pocket torn off of my wonderful sheepskin jacket. It cost me £70 – a lot of money in those days. This cop had wanted 10 dollars to show us in safely, but we thought he was joking. He wasn't and we ended up getting mobbed. That's police corruption for you!'

He recalled the fun of the Hamburg days. 'All the Hamburg kids had picked up English from the English bands. They all spoke with Scouse accents – and you should have heard the language. The funny thing was they didn't even realise they were swearing!'

As with many others, the Hamburg stint gave the Teens a hardened professional edge. The band had also backed Jerry Lee Lewis at the Stadt Hall in Berlin. The Teens witnessed star tantrums and became the victims when they proved a touch too honest for Jerry Lee Lewis. Sharp recalled: 'We were summoned to appear on a television spectacular with Jerry and Chuck Berry.'

The band played through several Lewis classics, such as *Great Balls Of Fire*, with no problems. But the problem came when he threw in Little Richard's *Good Golly Miss Molly*. The Teens had not realised Lewis did that number and that it had been on one of his albums. Worse still, his version was different from Richard's and drummer Barry Jenkins was caught out in an unexpected break. Lewis asked Barry why he was not familiar with his version and the drummer was honest enough to reply 'I'm not a fan'.

'That was it,' said Sharp. 'We were straight out on the street – kicked off the show.'

The Nashville Teens' usual gig fee in those days was £100–£125; maximum £150. Harris said, 'We would always be going off to see Don Arden in his office in Carnaby Street because he always owed us money. He would fob us off with a few quid. We had no choice. There were times when we didn't even have enough money to put petrol in the van to get to gigs.'

Tobacco Road had earned a fortune in 1964. But the fortune was not the Teens'. They were paid an unbelievably paltry seven eighths of a penny per single. Mickie Most was a talented producer, but he also had a talent for squeezing everything from his young protégés.

The song – discovered by Sharp – had catapulted the band to national fame. It was masterminded at the group's regular rehearsal venue – the George in Addlestone. 'It's still there,' said Sharp. 'I used to work in a record shop in Addlestone owned by a guy called Tom Ricketts. He was kind enough to let me borrow records to work on for the band. I found *Tobacco Road* and thought we could do that, but we'd need to speed it up.'

Harris said: 'We went into the Kingsway studio in Holborn where we used to record with Mickie, but my bass speaker was knackered. It was making a raspberry noise and I said You can't make a record like this. But Mickie, who was listening upstairs, said 'Actually, it sounds quite good', so we kept it in.'

Sharp added: 'We took several songs in that day and they hadn't been overly impressed. They said yeah, yeah, what else you got? We played them *Tobacco Road* and I looked up and Mickie looked up. They said That's it!'

Harris added: 'Mickie's big idea was he wanted us to hit a coke bottle with a screwdriver. That was his contribution. But of course he produced the record very well.'

With Don Arden guiding their career and Mickie Most producing the records, the Nashville Teens witnessed at first hand how tough the music business was. 'Don Arden was a bastard to everyone, but his missus took to Art, and so that was good for him,' recalled Harris.

The view the stars saw from the stage.
(*Aldershot News*)

Nashville Teens' Peter Harris, left, and Art Sharp, centre, pictured with fan and friend Martyn Wright at Mr Wright's home in the summer of 2006. (Author's collection)

'He once tried to sell us this pink Chevrolet. He said just drive that around town and everyone will think you're a star. Of course, it was a pile of crap.'

Art added: 'He always said, whatever you do, look like a star. Even if you can't afford it. Get a roller – look the part. We wouldn't have done the things we did without him.'

When Sharp left the band in 1972, it was to work for Arden, which he did for more than twenty years.

The Nashvilles are far from being teens these days, but they are the great survivors – and remain on good terms. Harris concluded: 'I was in the band for five years in the 1960s. We had our little moodies, just like anyone else, but we never stopped being friends.'

The band is still around today and singer Ray Phillips is still fronting. Before a gig at the Silver Birch pub in Bracknell on 16 April 2005, he recalled some of the grim realities of life as a pop star in 1960s Britain. 'We were paid seven eighths of a penny for every single sold. That's the deal we were on. I thought I was doing well earning £40 or so a week because my dad was earning a fiver!'

Ray also has his memories of Don Arden the hard man. 'I walked into his office once and one of his goons was dangling somebody from one of the bands out of the window by his feet. You didn't cross the guy for anything.'

My gangster cousin was the real Mister Big

The Small Faces' manager Don Arden had a reputation as one of the hardest men in the business. His autobiography was entitled *Mister Big* and that's how most people saw him. One notable exception was the laid-back, affable Small Faces' drummer Kenney Jones. He may not have been in the market for doing Arden any physical harm – but he knew several people who would not have batted an eyelid. Kenney recalled:

I was having a Sunday lunchtime drink with a cousin at a time when we were having some money trouble with Mr Arden. Where I came from, you got used to being around gangsters, and this cousin, who has since passed away, was one of the biggest hoods in the East End.

I casually mentioned our troubles involving Mr Arden to my cousin and my cousin said 'So that's it then. I'll kill him'. He meant it, too. It took a hell of a lot of persuading from me to stop him carrying out the threat.

Kenney, who went on to drum with the Faces and the Who, does not remember much about the Aldershot fiasco with the Hollies. 'We

Former Small Faces drummer Kenney Jones pictured at his Hurtwood Park Polo Club in Ewhurst. (Author's collection)

were great mates with the Hollies. If there was a conflict that night, it wouldn't have been brought on by us. It would have been Don Arden's big ego – you know, we should top the bill because we've just had a big hit.'

The Small Faces travelled in more comfort than some of their 1960s contemporaries. While other bands were condemned to a month or more of the rickety tour bus and damp bedsits, the Small Faces were lording it up in their very own Mark 10 Jaguar. 'We had this old guy who was our roadie – Bill Corbett his name was. He used to drive the Beatles until they sacked him for selling his story to the papers. I used to sit in the front and he'd freak out if any of us jumped up or mucked about.'

Even if it was an advantage, the Small Faces travelling in comfort, there was no escaping the mayhem when they finally arrived at venues. Kenney recalled:

All I remember is screaming girls and nutty situations. Our number one fan was a Geordie girl we dubbed Mad Ann. We finished one gig at Newcastle City Hall and we fought our way through the crowds and finally made it to the Jag. We pulled away and had gone some distance when I looked out of the window to see Mad Ann and her mate Sandy running alongside waving at us. I looked down at the speedo and we were doing 30mph!

In those days, we'd only play for about 20 minutes and we couldn't hear a thing. It was madness – all the screaming.

The frustrating thing about the Small Faces was that we could all play and yet we couldn't escape all that pop image stuff – the screaming girls and the hits.

After the Don Arden era we were with Andrew Oldham and he promised us unlimited studio time and I really found myself as a drummer. I began doing lots of session work. But when we were in Germany we picked up one of the music papers and discovered that he had gone into the studio and put out *Lazy Sunday*, a track we had only recorded for a laugh, as a single and that made the pop image even worse.

The Small Faces came from humble roots. They were East End boys – Kenney from Stepney, Steve Marriott from Ilford and Ronnie 'Plonk' Lane from East Ham, with Ian 'Mac' McLagan from Hounslow replacing original member Jimmy Winston. They had known hard times:

In the beginning I remember us driving up north and begging to do gigs. The van broke down in Knutsford of all places and we had to wait about for two days. We had threepence between us. I walked two miles into Knutsford village and I looked through this window at this rock cake. It was fourpence! We couldn't even afford that, but somehow I managed to persuade them to part with it and didn't eat it on the way back. The ceiling of our old van was rusty and I remember all this brown rust coming out when we washed our hair at one place.

We turned up at the Mojo club in Sheffield once. It was Peter Stringfellow's club. We were begging him to let us play if he'd feed us. Well we did play and we brought the house down. We did the deal with Don Arden soon after.

The band soon became flavour of the month. Their new flash mod gear may have made them scream idols for the girls – but you had to be brave to go out looking like that where they came from:

I remember wanting to go down the pub with my dad and I was there in my pink shirt or mauve trousers and he said 'You're not coming down the pub with me dressed like that'.

Kenney was only fifteen when the group signed with Arden and he was sixteen when their first record *Whatcha Gonna Do About It?* was released on Decca. 'We had a hit record when I was so young. Can you imagine being fifteen/sixteen and every girl is after you? The truth is, none of us were in it for the fame or fortune. It was just the music. And I never had a single drumming lesson.'

The band made their television debut on *Thank Your Lucky Stars* where they had the comfort zone of miming. Their second appearance was on *Ready Steady Go*, and they played live. Kenney said:

It was no problem for us. That's what we did. I always say that the Small Faces were the most creative and passionate band I played with because they were the first. The Faces were a fun-filled goodtime party band – great fun to be with – and the Who were one of the most exciting bands of all time.

The Small Faces had their little tiffs, but never in a way to upset the balance of what we were doing.

There were some hilarious incidents. One was in Berlin. We'd landed at the airport which was right in the middle of town. It was like having an airport at Piccadilly. Anyway, the four of us got in this cab and Steve Marriott wouldn't shut up. He kept going on, making all these Nazi jibes. There was still rubble from the war and if we drove past a building that hadn't been hit, he'd pipe up with 'Oh, we must have missed that one' – stuff like that. We got out on to the autobahn – in the middle of nowhere – and this German cabbie had had enough. He slung us all out and we had to hitch!

The Faces are still together – socially. 'We do a TV show every eight or nine years and I would still be up for doing a full Faces tour,' said Kenney. One thing missing, though, would be the hard drinking:

I still feel seventeen inside, and you can forget you're getting older. It takes me so much longer to get over a hangover now. I don't want to feel like that any more.

I finally got to do a gig at the Cavern in 2005 – after all those years. But I downed a bottle of bubbly because it was so hot in there and then coming out into the cold I got a bout of pneumonia.

I saw a programme on the Discovery Channel about the binge drinking epidemic and how teenagers are getting cirrhosis of the liver. And binge drinking is considered to be having more than three drinks in an hour. There comes a time in life when you have to settle for moderation.

Kenney now owns the Hurtwood Park polo club in Ewhurst, and is actively involved in it. He loves the sport and Princes Charles and Harry are among the esteemed visitors.

Rock royalty also visit: Ringo Starr lives nearby and is a welcome visitor, as is Kenney's pal Paul Weller. According to Kenney:

He's unbelievable. He is such a fan of what we did and is so curious about it all. He'll be firing questions – what was it like and so on, like he's interviewing me. I'm proud to know that the Small Faces were such a big influence on him.

The joyful faces of the fans as they greet their heroes.
(*Aldershot News*)

Ringo is great too. I get to spend just about every Christmas with him. We were all fans of the Beatles.

David Essex, Pete Townshend and Moody Blue John Lodge are also good pals picked up along the way.

Kenney's latest band – the Jones Gang, featuring Robert Hart, Rick Wills and Kenney – have brought the drummer full circle. In 2005, exactly forty years since his first hit single, the band hit the American billboard charts with their single *Angel* from their album *Any Minute Now.*

Forty years after stepping out on those early UK tours, Kenney is doing it all over again. This time it's New Zealand, Australia, America and South Africa on the horizon. In late June 2007, looking back on those crazy package tour days of the 1960s, he said, 'They were like mini Live Aids, those gigs, to have so many stars all playing on one night. They were very special and really set the scene for what was to come after.'

Jaywalking into the limelight

Peter Jay and the Jaywalkers had limited chart success, but they were right at the heart of the 1960s touring scene; by the time they were in Aldershot in October 1966 on the Hollies package, they were already veteran performers.

Drummer Peter Jay, who now owns a string of entertainment venues in Great Yarmouth, recalled:

We started out in 1962 working for Larry Parnes, playing the circuit with guys like Billy Fury, Marty Wilde and Eden Kane. We toured with the Beatles in 1964 and the Rolling Stones in 1966. The Stones tour also featured Ike and Tina Turner and the Yardbirds. Long John Baldry was the compère – he wasn't even singing.

Life on the road may have had its moments, but it certainly wasn't lucrative:

Our usual fee was about £20 a week each – and out of that we had to pay our digs! I don't think anyone made any money. Everybody got ripped off. The only ones who ended up making anything were those who survived for at least five years – long enough to set up publishing companies and management for themselves.

Even the brightest hopefuls were constantly short of cash:

Two things I remember about the Small Faces on that Hollies tour were first how good they were, and second how skint they always were.

Peter Jay, third from the right, with his Jaywalkers. (Courtesy of Peter Jay)

I vividly remember them always coming to borrow money off us. It'd be 'lend us a tenner'.

Life on the road was unrelenting:

You just got completely exhausted. Sometimes you'd be touring for months and if you got sick you just had to carry on. If you were lucky enough to get a day off, you'd just sleep. And of course, we had the setting up to do as well. For most bands, it wasn't just a matter of turning up to play. You'd have to drive home if you were near enough. If not, it was back to the digs then up early the next day for the bus.

Touring with the Beatles was an eye-opener:

One time in Glasgow, we got trapped in our van for more than an hour. We got besieged because we were seen getting in and they thought the Beatles were in there. We had to be rescued in the end. They brought in police horses to free the van up.

It was mayhem at times outside the stage door. The problem was the girls would go mad up the front and then the lads at the back would get the needle and start putting the boot in.

The adrenalin-fuelled excitement of the concerts more than made up for the endless hours on the road and the uncomfortable B&B:

It was all great fun, and there was always the expectation of what might happen. It sounds daft now, but when you toured with the Beatles and they were topping the bill, at the back of your mind you were thinking, it will be us next year.

It wasn't until we played Bournemouth, and CBS sent film crews over from America just to interview the Beatles that we thought – hang on a minute, there's something much bigger going on here. Up until then, if you made it big it meant you might go to Europe because you had sold some records in Germany, France or Holland.

Despite the rock 'n' roll lifestyle, there was still routine:

Of course, we mainly travelled on the tour bus. We all used to meet near Baker Street underground station in Seymour Place because everyone lived in London back then. We didn't have a PA or big sound systems to take around – we'd roll up at the venue and just use the house equipment. The sound must have been awful. It would just be a crap PA and you would have to try to make yourselves heard over all that screaming and shouting.

Even on the Beatles tour it was the same. It seems unbelievable now. On tour with the Beach Boys was the first time I'd seen a mixing desk. They operated it from down in the orchestra pit. It's funny, even the humblest local band has all that stuff now, but it wasn't like that then – even for the biggest stars.

Chart success passed Peter Jay and the Jaywalkers by. The nearest they got was their first single, *Can Can*, an important part of their stage act. It crept into the charts in November 1962, and stuck around for eleven weeks, peaking at 19. 'Looking back, we just didn't make the right records,' said Peter. 'We were more of a live band really. A good stage act.'

However, Peter Jay and the Jaywalkers played an unwitting part in one of the most important songs of the 1960s. He explained:

On that Hollies tour in 1966, we got the added job of providing the backing for Paul Jones who had just split from Manfred Mann. We backed Paul for months. But he wanted an organist to create the right sound for the Manfred Mann numbers and we settled on a guy called Matthew Fisher.

The problem was he started to drive us mad by constantly playing this piece of classical music – Bach I think it was – whenever we were rehearsing and it got on our nerves so much that we sacked him in the end.

You can imagine our reaction about six months later after he got together with Procol Harum and they released this song called *Whiter Shade Of Pale* built around this piece of classical music.

Peter Jay in 2006.
(Courtesy of Peter Jay)

Of course, I loved the record, but I always just think of Matthew Fisher when I hear it.

Ultimately, there were good and bad decisions. One of the good decisions was taken by Peter's drumming pal Bobby Elliott:

Bobby was a fantastic drummer. He was working with Shane Fenton and the Fentones and then he told me one day that he was leaving to join this Manchester band called the Hollies. I remember they had suits like the Beatles, only theirs had a square cut neck. I thought he was mad. I was so shocked that he was leaving Shane, who had been successful, to join them – but what a decision it proved to be!

One decision – unbeknown to Peter and his Jaywalkers – was to have a very adverse effect on their future:

We had toured with the Beatles and they offered us a place on their Christmas show at the Astoria that ran for about three weeks. What we didn't know was that our agent tried to get them to up the money by about £200 a week for the band and they said no and offered the gig to our rivals, Sounds Incorporated, instead.

Sounds Incorporated, like us, were mainly an instrumental band, and they got to tour America with the Beatles after that, culminating in that famous gig at Shea Stadium. We'd have done it for nothing!

Jay has memories of Jimi Hendrix when he came to London:

I first saw him in the Scotch of St James Club. We were upstairs when someone said you've got to come down, there's this guy playing the guitar with his teeth. It was amazing. Jimi quickly moved on to play at the bigger Speakeasy and we watched him there too and spent time with him. He was a lovely, gentle bloke.

It was the early days of the motorways and musicians would often meet up at the Blue Boar café on the M1: 'You would see them all in there when they were touring – the Beatles, the Stones. But our guitarist was excited when he saw Chuck Berry in there one day. He was like a god to him.'

Peter Jay and the Jaywalkers, made up of Peter Miller (lead guitar), Tony Webster (rhythm), Mac McIntyre (tenor saxophone/flute), Lloyd Baker (baritone saxophone/piano), Johnny Larke (bass), Geoff Moss (six-string bass) and, of course, Peter Jay on drums, finally called it a day in 1969.

Drumming obviously runs in the Jay family: 'My youngest son Jack plays and he's excellent – a lot better than I ever was. He's technically gifted, but I just used to wave my arms about a lot to make up for the stuff I couldn't do!'

The mum and daughter who saw every show

Jane Sylvester was one lucky little girl. Not only did her mum Pat love pop music, but she regularly took her to concerts – including all seven at the ABC in Aldershot.

The one that sticks out was the 1966 show headlined by Jane's favourites, the Hollies. It was certainly memorable for the then eleven-year-old Jane who ended up sitting on the stage while Hollie Allan Clarke sang to her and held her hand.

Jane did not have to worry about persuading her pals at St Nicholas School in Fleet that it really happened, for the moment was captured in a photograph published in that week's *New Musical Express*. 'I still have the cutting,' said Jane. 'It's my most treasured possession!'

Pat said:

We had front row seats, right in the middle – we invariably did, because I used to send a cheque off straight away. We were able to stay in our seats and see everything for most of the show, but everything changed when the Hollies came on. Girls from all round the auditorium ran forward beyond the control of the security people.

Because Jane was so young and was getting trampled underfoot a security guard lifted her on to the stage. He said it was the only safe place he could put her, and I spent the rest of the Hollies' performance standing in front of her and pushing away those teenagers who would just trample anybody to get up on the stage.

The *NME* picture clearly captures worried mum in front of Jane who was clad in a yellow Tartan waistcoat and skirt and perched happily on the stage being serenaded by her idols. Jane said:

I remember the Hollies made quite a fuss of me and Allan Clarke came and held my hand and then sang a song to me. Tony Hicks smiled at me too. He was my favourite.

We had met them before when mum took us up to see Cliff at the Talk of the Town in London and the Hollies were in the audience. One or two were a bit the worse for wear but Tony was great and gave me his autograph. He had such a sweet, kind face. He was a brilliant musician, but the quiet one on stage.

Seeing my picture in the *NME* that week was marvellous and I remember showing some of my friends at school and they were quite amused. I didn't show the teachers, though!

Another enduring memory was of one of the Ryan brothers putting his foot through the stage at the front and almost toppling over.

Jane was ten when she was taken to the first Aldershot ABC concert, starring Del Shannon and Herman's Hermits – but that was not her first concert. Mother and daughter remember going to see Joe Brown and the Bruvvers at a cinema in Haslemere some time before that.

The Sylvester family lived and worked on their Freelands Farm in Gally Hill Road, Church Crookham. The wooden walls of the shed where they sorted the eggs were littered with colour posters from Jane's pop magazines, while the radio blared out the latest sounds.

Jane, who sported a Cathy McGowan hairstyle – long with a fringe – would always be taken to the 6.15 p.m. shows because she had to be in bed early for school and mum was up at the crack of dawn working on the farm. Pat said:

We took my farm helper Pat Champion with us that night as a treat because she was a huge fan of Del Shannon. All she would talk about was what lovely thighs he had! He was absolutely brilliant. It was the only time I ever saw him. We enjoyed Herman's Hermits too. They were very popular.

The Roy Orbison show in 1967 was another highlight. Pat recalled:

Roy Orbison was excellent. He sang some of his hits and I'm fairly sure he had two drummers that night. We were big fans of the Searchers too and they played *Needles And Pins* that night.

The generation game: fans of all ages sat happily together. (*Aldershot News*)

Mum and daughter were there for the Walkers, of course. Pat confessed:

We were sitting on the right-hand side about four rows from the front, but we weren't big fans of Jimi. I found his music a bit disturbing, although I did admire his guitar playing. I was fascinated by him playing the guitar behind his back. I think he had a yellow shirt on – for that performance anyway. We would have been excited about seeing the Walkers – Scott especially. I remember seeing them and all the screaming!

Mum and daughter are still close. These days Jane – now Jane Ash – lives near her parents, just a few hundred yards up the road in Crookham Village.

Five
Gene Pitney and the Troggs

Love Is All Around on the Troggs tour with Gene

ALWAYS THOUGHT OF as the kiss of death for any pop star's career – American heart-throb Gene Pitney broke the golden rule by marrying his childhood sweetheart, Lynn Gayton, shortly before his tour with the Troggs kicked off at the Astoria in Finsbury Park on Friday 17 February 1967. The debate in the music papers leading up to the tour centred on how Pitney's new status as a married man would go down with the fans.

The Troggs, fresh off a tour with the Walker Brothers and their screaming teenyboppers, were relieved to be touring with someone whose fans were of a more mature nature.

Gene bounced into Britain ready for the gruelling slog of one-nighters that included dates in Ireland, Scotland and Wales. His backing band were the experienced and capable Sounds Incorporated, whose standing in the industry had been cemented in August 1965 when they were filmed as a support act to the Beatles at Shea Stadium.

Pitney, who celebrated his twenty-sixth birthday on that opening night, put in his usual professional performance, winning praise from music columnists as he churned out the hits and he found time to read out some birthday greetings on stage.

The Troggs, with their younger fan base, certainly attracted their share of attention, leaping on stage in a rather unusual combination of white jackets and orange trousers. Making up the rest of the bill for the tour were Australian singer Normie Rowe with his backing band the Playboys, singer David Garrick, a band called the Vision and finally the Loot who, like the Troggs, hailed from Andover and whose line-up included ex-Trogg David Wright. The compère holding this lot together was Bryan Burdon.

Gene Pitney gives it his all on stage as the security guards keep a wary eye on the girls. (*Aldershot News*)

Pitney's fears of how the fans would react to his marriage vanished after the early shows at the big cities, with the Odeon Birmingham and the Liverpool Empire following the opening night. The star, who had been wondering whether to halt his appearances in the UK for a while, changed his mind rapidly on the strength of his welcome. He also took delight in the success of the Troggs who were earning cheers from fans and praise from the critics.

The next week took the tour on to the ABC at Gloucester, the Wolverhampton Gaumont, the ABC at Lincoln, the Hull ABC, Newcastle City Hall, the ABC Blackpool and the De Montfort Hall, Leicester, without a break.

The pattern was becoming clear by now – applause for Pitney, a wild reaction for the Troggs, and a struggle for the rest.

The Loot opened with a 10-minute spot. Reg Presley was largely responsible for their big break on the tour, but it didn't work out for them. There was criticism that they were just clones of the Troggs and they were not having the problem of their tiny sets being drowned out by screaming.

Australian Rowe, backed by the Playboys, was on next, but he fared little better. Normie was big news back home where he had racked up a string of hits, but he was unknown in the UK. He had been a recording artist since 1965, specialising in giving a 'Merseybeat' twist to classic old songs like *Que Sera Sera*, *It Ain't Necessarily So* and *I Who Have Nothing*. The formula worked Down Under with singles EPs and LPs all charting; however, the Merseybeat-era had already been consigned to history in the UK and Normie's career never took off in Britain.

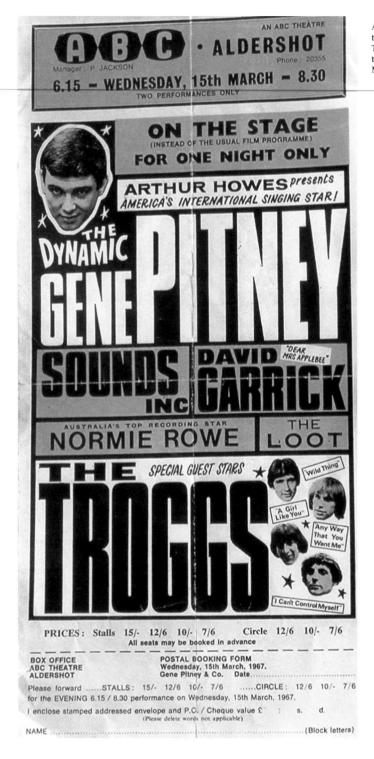

A 1967 handbill from the Gene Pitney/Troggs appearance at the Aldershot ABC in March 1967.

David Garrick was yet another Scouser who headed for London in the mid-1960s in search of fame and fortune. Garrick, however, had a background in opera singing. His first two singles bombed before he was handed the Jagger/Richards song *Lady Jane* in the summer of 1966, but it peaked at twenty-eight. The follow up, *Dear Mrs Applebee*, did only slightly better, reaching twenty-two. Other artists on the tour were giving Garrick a boost with regular favourable mentions in the music press, but it did not do the trick. He never managed to find that elusive hit.

Wolverhampton Express and *Star* pop critic John Ogden was particularly taken with Pitney's performance and remarked that the Troggs were a much-improved live act, with guitarist Chris Britton and singer/songwriter Presley drawing praise. Normie Rowe's latest single *I Don't Care, Show Me Where* was thrown in, but all the attention was falling on the headline acts.

Monday 27 February represented a day off to recover – and Mondays continued to be the day off for the rest of the tour – so there was a chance to give the tonsils a break before the slog resumed at the ABC Chester and the Manchester Odeon on the Tuesday and Wednesday, before a trip over the border to the Glasgow Odeon and the ABC Edinburgh on the following two nights. The ABC Stockton and the Odeon, Leeds, hosted the next two nights to round off the week.

It was certainly gruelling. Pitney went to see a London doctor to help maintain his voice, but he was still enjoying himself. The tour was playing to decent houses up and down the country and there was soon a new member on the tour. The Troggs were given a Labrador when the show hit Edinburgh and the band took the dog everywhere.

There was plenty of goodwill between all the acts with frequent complimentary comments about each other in the music papers. Even compère Burdon got a mention when Pitney told one newspaper: 'Bryan, who features in your *Pinky and Perky* TV show, is doing a difficult job really well. It's no joke trying to make jokes when the fans want to see the singers, but Bryan's working real hard.'

The next week's schedule was ridiculous, even by the crazy standards of the era. The Adelphi at Slough hosted the Tuesday show and then the package headed to Ireland for shows at the ABC Belfast and the Adelphi in Dublin before finishing the week back in London for dates at the Granada in East Ham and the Odeon at Hammersmith. They then headed out to Suffolk for the Sunday date at the Gaumont in Ipswich.

The exhausted stars were now heading for their final week and there were some signs of tension amongst the Troggs.

Presley threatened to pull out after a series of microphone failures at key moments. He told a reporter:

It's very unfair on both the group and the fans. At Ipswich last night the mike went dead half-way through the act and I got so furious I just threw it on the stage. It was just about the end.

There are regulations saying that an alternative mike should be ready at the side of the stage so that if anything goes wrong you can just reach out and get it. But often it isn't set up and by the time they've got it ready, you've finished.

Looking back all these years later, Presley believes the duff microphones episode was probably down to a little bit of sabotage:

It used to go on. People would do things to try to ruin your act – whether it was jealousy or whatever. But it kept happening to us and it was always in the build-up to an important part and I remember getting the microphone that night and throwing it down in a bit of a temper. I was testing all the mikes and making quite a case out of it, but it worked. It never happened again.

So the Troggs played on. The next date was the Colston Hall at Bristol on Tuesday 14 March, and the following night the show rolled into Aldershot to play at the ABC Cinema. The Troggs got the all-star scream treatment from the fans this night.

It was the familiar scenario by now: hordes of girls, beside themselves with excitement, storming the stage while the line of hired bouncers stood equally determined to repel the invaders before the star turns were torn limb from limb.

The bouncers did not always win. The Troggs launched into *Wild Thing* and the crowd obviously took it as a hint. Fans thronged the aisle and surrounded the stage. Although most were kept at bay by the bouncers, one lucky girl got through, managing to embrace Presley. Well, lucky for a few seconds until the bouncers moved in for Round Two!

The Troggs carried on belting out their hits, including, ironically, *I Can't Control Myself*, a big hit for them six months before. They also played their current song *Give It To Me*. Pandemonium greeted each hit, with the screams growing louder and the fans more wild. By their final number, more than 100 girls had left their seats to group around the stage. The bouncers were to earn their money this night.

Photographs captured the mayhem as Presley held sway, first with the microphone and then with a guitar at his hip, as he stirred up the excitement.

Mercifully, the Troggs were not torn limb from limb that night and Presley lived to tell the tale. He achieved fame again in 1994 when Wet Wet Wet recorded his song *Love Is All Around* for the film *Four Weddings and a Funeral*, staying at the top of the charts for fifteen weeks. It made him a millionaire overnight. Not bad for a song he wrote in a quarter of an hour almost three decades before.

The atmosphere was a lot calmer when bill-topper Gene Pitney took the stage later in the evening, backed by Sounds Incorporated. By 1967 Pitney had already chalked up a succession of hits, including nine that had made the Top Ten. But his current song, *Cold Light Of Day*, which had entered the charts three weeks before, was not one of the best and only reached a disappointing thirty-four.

Now to clear up a misunderstanding – nearly four decades on. Accompanying the review of the concert in the *Aldershot News* came a

Screaming for the Troggs. (*Aldershot News*)

report that the Troggs had visited a local second-hand shop to buy some military uniforms to wear on stage. They were all the rage for mods at the time and the story went that the Troggs and support act Sounds Incorporated took the opportunity to deck themselves out in some authentic gear while they were in the home of the British Army.

It was reported that before the first performance they went round to trader Terry Grey's junk shop in Gordon Road and after rummaging around for some time gathered together about £15-worth of old uniforms, hats, fur coats and military signs. Trader Grey, needless to say, was delighted by this nod of approval. 'We didn't recognise them at first, but they seemed nice lads,' he said. 'These military uniforms are certainly selling well at the moment. You can hardly get into the shop on Saturday mornings with all the local youngsters in here buying the mod gear.'

However, it can now be revealed that it probably was not the Troggs who bought all that swinging mod gear that day, but the Loot. Presley said:

I'd be almost certain it was them. I know it wasn't us. The Loot were a local band and we'd got them on the tour to try to help them along a little bit. However, they broke up shortly after the tour.

It's the sort of stuff they would have gone for. In fact, I vaguely remember them in some military type stuff after the show.

Other Aldershot businessmen had cause to thank the performers for their custom that night. After the show, Sounds Incorporated spent the night at the South Western Hotel in Station Road while the Troggs reportedly bedded down at the George Hotel in Wellington Street, now called the Goose. 'It's a mystery why we did that,' said Presley. 'After all, Aldershot's not far from Andover and we were travelling in our Humber Super Snipe by then, so we would normally have gone home. Perhaps we were playing in London the next night?'

In fact, the tour moved on to the Guildhall at Portsmouth that Thursday night, before heading off to the Winter Gardens at Bournemouth the next night, the Capitol at Cardiff on the Saturday before the final night at the Coventry Theatre on Sunday 19 March.

Troggs and slogs – life on the road in the 1960s

Reg Presley summed up the 1960s pop package tour in a single word – frenzied:

We were young, and it was fun, but I couldn't work at that pace now. I'd last about a week. We would all travel together on the bus and the schedules were so tight that you would pull up at the hotel and you would only have an hour for a quick shave and shower before you had to dash off to the venue. And that's how it went on, day after day.

All the screaming meant you struggled to hear anything. I remember going to see the Rolling Stones at the Gaumont in Southampton and the only song I could make out was *The Last Time* – and we were about two feet from the stage.

In those days, the kids didn't really come to hear you. They came to see you – to touch you if they could, and they got carried away with it all and that's why there was all the screaming. They would grab your legs and there was a real danger you would get pulled down into the audience. That's when you were grateful for the bouncers to give you some protection.

And you didn't have the gear they have now. You'd have a small PA and of course it wasn't enough. But it was very exciting to be up there. Kind of like walking on the moon. It's funny, when we go out now and you look down and there are sixteen and seventeen year olds, and if

(*Above*) **Excited scenes at the Aldershot ABC.** (*Aldershot News*)

(*Right*) **Note the excited girls at the front getting ready to make a lunge for Trogg Reg Presley.** (*Aldershot News*)

(*Opposite*) **Reg Presley with the guitar around his neck as the Troggs rocked on – it was just a prop, he confessed.** (*Aldershot News*)

THE TROGGS

Love is still all around them... The Troggs in 2006. (Courtesy of Reg Presley)

I forget the words they are all singing them and I can pick it up from them. They know all the lyrics!

Hard work though they were, those one-nighters were invaluable for plugging that all-important new single:

It was a showcase. You got to play your best stuff and show people what you could do. Then, hopefully, you could maybe go back with your own show and perhaps just one other band and do your own thing.

Presley recalled that the final night of the tours could be unpredictable:

I'm sure it was the final night of that tour when someone got a steak and kidney pie shoved in their face. That's the sort of thing that would happen on the last night. It was over and people didn't have to be nice to you any more! I can't remember who caught the pie in the face – it was so long ago. It might even have been me, but it was typical of what would go on.

In true showbiz style, all the stars might gather on stage at the end for a grand finale – providing they were getting along well enough:

We'd have a drink together and then it would be cheerio, see you next time and we would all go our separate ways. But it wasn't always as wild as they made out. You know with *Wild Thing* they presumed that it was like that, but it wasn't really. But you know how it is with most of the press. You tell them something and they imagine the rest.

Wild times or not, the 1960s treadmill could take its toll on your health:

We had all our hits in the first 18 months. We'd put out something and then while it was still in the charts we would have to put another one out. That's how our management seemed to like it. We'd have preferred to have a gap of about six months like they do now. Having said that, they don't really sell singles any more, do they? I don't know how the future is going to pan out. If the internet becomes all legal and above board with a bigger range of music and people get their royalties, fine. But if they don't and people's stuff gets ripped off for nothing, I can see them not making music any more. I'm just glad we had our success when we did.

Back in the 1960s, the trouble was that they over-booked you. I'll give you an example. We did a three-week tour of Germany, and that's two shows every night, and then as soon as we got back we were straight on to live TV on *Ready Steady Go*. I never had a voice. I'd blown it on the tour. I spent most of the day in Harley Street with this man spraying some sort of ice powder on my throat just so I could talk! I said 'I can't do this'. They overworked you and then you had to have treatment from the doctor. The guy told me, don't let this happen again. When you are not singing, stop talking. You have to give your voice a chance to recover when you are a singer. Don't forget, you might have a 5-hour road journey after a gig and if you're talking all the time, you might not have a voice left the next day.

That's what I tell them today. You must learn to keep your mouth shut if you want to work.

Fortunately, Presley and the Troggs are still working today – and at a pace set by them. Original lead guitarist Chris Britton is still in the band, with Dave Maggs on drums and Pete Lucas on bass.

Thanks to the fortune earned from *Love Is All Around*, Presley can perform today because he enjoys it – not because he has to:

I'd heard it on the grapevine that they were going to do that song for the film. Then this cassette dropped on my mat one day. When I heard the opening with all those heavy chords, I thought woah, that's a bit more powerful than our quiet beginning. Then when I heard that voice I thought Wow! I loved it. I thought they brought the whole thing up to date.

Your songs are like your children really. You hope that people look after them properly, and that version was wonderful. They did a great job.

Ripping night when Gene went through the stage

Gene Pitney recalled the excitement of those 1960s tours in an interview just two weeks before his untimely death in the middle of a UK tour in April 2006. He recalled:

Those tours were great fun. It was a fantastic time to be young and out there playing music. We were just young guys having a great time. I remember all of the guys from that 1967 tour with the Troggs and Sounds Incorporated. It was a wonderful tour and the MC, Bryan Burdon, became a great friend and we worked together for several years.

I can remember Aldershot. My tour manager Ron King explained to me beforehand that Aldershot was the home of the army and that they did basic training there. After the soundcheck in the afternoon I was taken out to do a photo-shoot for the *Fab 208* magazine. We went out of the cinema and off down a windy road and the pictures were taken on a stone bridge over a river.

It's shocking to look back at the pictures. Just look at how crude the theatres were, and the sound systems were dreadful. I'm still wearing

Only one yard away from your arms... Gene Pitney stokes up the screams. (*Aldershot News*)

my suit, you can see. I'm sure that the guy in the white suit you can see singing in front of the band is Lucas of Lucas and the Mike Cotton Sound who often backed me on these tours.

Gene had a reputation as a likeable gentleman, happy to hear (and tell) bad jokes and take part in card games to while away the long hours on the bus. If he was not happy to be a victim of last-night pranks, such as being covered in foam by Status Quo on the finale of his 1968 tour, he took it with good grace and still appeared on stage on time, looking and sounding as good as ever. He was also not averse to putting his hand in his pocket to pay for everyone's lunch.

The Troggs tour was one that stood in his memory:

It was a great tour. The Troggs could party, but I had my moments too. There would be tricks played as well. I was all for that unless it was something that was going to ruin your performance – that was too much. Billy J. Kramer's band, the Dakotas, used to go in for that sort

Gene Pitney relaxes in his dressing room at the Aldershot ABC on his tour with the Troggs in March 1967. (*Aldershot News*)

of thing and so did Gerry and the Pacemakers. I used to travel on the coach and you got to know everybody. You lived with these guys on tour and a lot of friendships were made.

Of course, there would be the odd disaster:

The orchestra pits would be covered up for the pop shows – sometimes with just a black cloth. One night, I can't remember where it was, there was this great rip and I went straight through it. I was very lucky. I landed right on the organ. I just had to clamber back to my feet, smile and carry on singing.

It was back then that I started reading out messages on stage. It was a pretty unique thing, but it all started by accident. A fan sent me a card and I thought it was so funny that I would read it out on stage. Then other people gave me their cards to read out and before I knew it I was getting sackfuls.

Gene had first appeared in the UK at the back end of 1963 when *Twenty-Four Hours From Tulsa* was riding high in the charts:

I was supposed to be doing a tour of Mecca ballrooms. I had a song out called *Mecca* at the time and some brilliant agent thought it would make a perfect tie-in to play the Mecca venues. But when I got here the record company implied very strongly that they weren't suitable for my kind of music. Luckily, the promoter had got a few things wrong and I was able to wriggle out of the contract.

I did appear on four shows, though, to do *Twenty-Four Hours From Tulsa*. They were *Thank Your Lucky Stars* in Birmingham, *Top Of The Pops* and *Ready Steady Go* in London and *Disc A Go-Go*, which covered the south-west.

In those days, if you played those four shows and had a half decent song, you had a hit on your hands.

That song was the one that allowed me to go out of America. It was a great song written especially for me by Burt Bacharach and Hal David. They could pinpoint your strengths and weaknesses and structured the song for you. They were great talents.

Gene noted two major differences in touring today, compared with the 1960s:

The quality of the theatres is one. We played the old ABC, Odeon and Empire cinemas. Also, the roads. Back then there was only one motorway – the M1 – so whether you were going north, south, east or west you inevitably ended up going through all these side roads through towns all over the place, and you couldn't stay in one location.

His death on 5 April 2006, following a sell-out gig at St David's Hall, Cardiff, two weeks after this interview, robbed the world of a unique talent. Gene received a standing ovation after that final performance

The author with the late Gene Pitney in March 2006.
(Author's collection)

and he will be particularly missed in Britain where his large army of fans remained loyal.

When the sad news of his death was announced it brought back memories of a telephone conversation we had the previous month, shortly before he left the USA for the tour. He had spoken of his fitness regime and his determination to carry on for as long as possible. A month-long schedule as gruelling as the 1960s tours held no fears for him. He told me, 'I hate it when people say isn't it time you put your feet up? That's when you die. As long as I'm fit enough to still put everything into it and I'm still enjoying it, I'll carry on.'

The music business will miss him.

Roy Orbison, in his trademark dark glasses, surrounded by admirers at the Ipswich Gaumont in 1967. (*East Anglian Daily Times*)

Six
Roy Orbison Tour

The O must go on!

ROY ORBISON'S THIRTY-DATE tour with the Small Faces in the spring of 1967 suffered some devastating blows from the very beginning, with poor ticket sales, lukewarm reviews – the music press seemed to be going through a 'let's take a pot-shot at Orbison' phase with complaints that his laid-back style was boring – and a major star walking out after the opening night. It was some achievement that the show stayed the course and made it to the final night at Romford a little over three weeks later.

The opening night at the Finsbury Park Astoria, on Friday 3 March 1967, proved a personal disaster for Jeff Beck, who had quit the Yardbirds just a few months before to launch a solo career. How he must have regretted it that night! After suffering problems with his equipment he was jeered by some sections of the audience and one reviewer wrote witheringly: 'Breakaway Yardbird Jeff Beck must have learned an important lesson after failing miserably to make the grade in his own right.' This was a harsh and hasty judgement on a fine guitarist whose luck was to change, but he walked out after that opening night and was replaced by P.P. Arnold (a former backing singer for Ike and Tina Turner) with this explanation for fans:

There were a lot of reasons. First, the power for my amplifier was switched off. People may not have noticed it, but I did. Then somebody damaged it and I have to pay for it.

It's not worth appearing on a bill starring such names as Roy Orbison and the Small Faces. You're just playing to fans of these acts. It's a waste of time trying to get across.

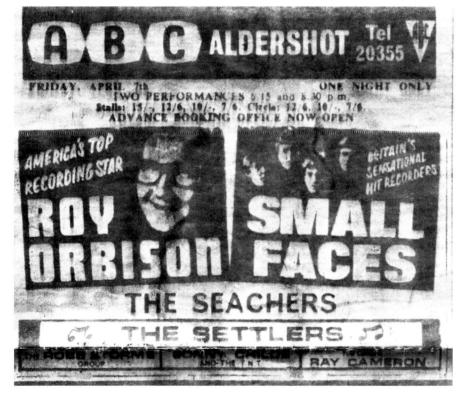

The advertisement for the Orbison package as it appeared in the *Aldershot News* a month before the show.

It was quite a comedown after appearing with the Yardbirds. I also understood my record *Hi-Ho Silver Lining* was being released to coincide with the tour, but it was held up through some technical hitch. So that was a waste.

Although Beck was cursing his luck that night, the Small Faces and Paul and Barry Ryan fared much better. The frenzied reaction of their fans covered up any frailties in their performance. It was pandemonium as the Small Faces were introduced, with girls crying and screaming and surging towards the stage, with pictures, banners and flags (those not confiscated by the management) waving. All manner of objects were thrown on the stage, including several handbags. Mix in amplifiers at full throttle over the screaming and it was not a gig for the purist.

The hysteria had not reached rows three to six which had been allocated to members of Roy Orbison's fan club. They were far more orderly, waiting politely for their man to appear.

The soulful ten-piece Sonny Childe and the TNT had opened the show, followed by Birmingham folksters the Settlers. Next it was the turn of the luckless Beck, before the Small Faces, to the wails of the teen army, completed the first half. Robb Storme and the Whispers started the second half, with the Ryan brothers following them, their delicate harmonies lost in the screams.

Orbison fans got a taste of what was to come as his backing group, the Candy Men appeared on stage for a spot of their own. Then it was time for the smiling Big O, behind his sunglasses and dressed immaculately in a smart black shirt and trousers. He was greeted with prolonged applause, rather than tears of hysteria.

However, he too had to battle to make himself heard as he opened with *Only The Lonely*, followed by *Lana*, *Too Soon To Know* and his latest record, *So Good*. The single struggled for airplays and reached only as high as thirty-two, staying in the charts for just six weeks. He then sang *Leah* and *Mean Woman Blues* before finishing with two blockbusters, *It's Over* and *Pretty Woman*.

In the audience on that opening night were Jonathan King and Walker Brother Scott Engel. The night finished on a high for Orbison, who attended a midnight charity show in London and was greeted by Princess Margaret. Despite this, the raggedness of the show did not go down well with critics. Tickets were not selling well and this had a knock-on effect for other tours. Days later the Kingsway Theatre in Hadleigh, Essex, cancelled their Hendrix/Cat Stevens/Walkers/Humperdinck date for the following month because they had made such big losses on the Orbison/Small Faces night, with only 350 attending the first house. Some Orbison tickets had the wrong date printed on them, which hardly helped.

The Orbison tour continued to be dogged by patchy sales, but after that worrying opening night the sets got tighter as the tour bus wended its merry way into Exeter the next night, followed by Plymouth, Birmingham, Bolton, Manchester, Chesterfield, Liverpool,

Roy Orbison, like all good pop stars, was happy to sign for fans. (*Aldershot News*)

Luton, Southampton, Tooting, Wolverhampton and Newcastle. Orbison found time before the Birmingham show for a tour of the local BSA factory to admire the motorbikes.

The Wolverhampton show was a good one for the Settlers, who were playing virtually on their home patch. The trio, who met at college in Birmingham, got plenty of respectful applause, and they had the added bonus of their set not being drowned out by screams. They threw in their latest single *On The Other Side*.

A breakdown on the road meant the Small Faces were late and they went on immediately before show-closer Orbison in the first house. This was uncomfortable for Roy as the teens were screaming for the Londoners right up until he walked on stage. However, he soon won them over and hit them with his classic encore of *Pretty Woman* to finish on a high.

Paul and Barry Ryan attracted their share of the screams, but the rest of the bill were struggling for attention, although the voice of P.P. Arnold was inspiring.

Some of the guys got a rest for a few nights when Orbison and the Small Faces did a small Scottish detour of their own, appearing at the Edinburgh ABC on 20 March, the Glasgow Odeon on 21 March and the Carlisle ABC on 22 March. The others then rejoined the package, rolling on and on through Leeds, Doncaster, Lincoln, Coventry, Blackpool, Cardiff, Bristol and Cheltenham to end the month.

Without a break, the show then moved on to Bournemouth, Leicester, Ipswich and Slough, before reaching Aldershot. Paul and Barry Ryan had now quit the tour to play some dates in Australia, flying out on 7 April – the date the tour reached Aldershot. At least there was a quality replacement in the Searchers, who played Aldershot and the tour's final date at Romford two nights later.

A local review of the Aldershot show was headlined 'Cinema Half-Full For Orbison Show'. However, the bad news ended there. The Aldershot few gave the stars an enthusiastic welcome, and at least the Small Faces appeared this time – their misdemeanours of the previous

(*Left*) **Sonny Childe and TNT put in a dynamite performance.** (*Aldershot News*)

(*Right*) **Sonny Childe, aka R.B. Greaves, keeps his balance despite the TNT explosion.** (*Aldershot News*)

year now forgiven, if not forgotten. Steve Marriott enthused: 'A great reception. They just stood up and dug the music!'

P.P. Arnold opened the show with the Supremes song *You Keep Me Hanging On*. The audience were already clapping and singing along. She followed that up with Georgie Fame's wistful *I'm Ready For Love*. She was followed by the Settlers – a trio comprising banjo player John Fyffe, singer/tambourinist Cindy Kent and guitarist Mike Jones – who picked their way through *Cotton Fields*, *Always On My Mind* and the Lennon and McCartney classic *Nowhere Man*.

Sonny Childe and TNT then exploded onto the stage with a succession of soul numbers, inevitably including *Midnight Hour*, plus *You Don't Know Like I Know* and *Satisfaction*.

Compère Ray Cameron stepped into the spotlight for the big build-up and then it was the familiar scene of screaming girls crowding round the stage for their mod heroes the Small Faces, who closed the first half. From the first few bars of their opening number – Sam Cooke's *Shake* – the screaming was deafening. Over

the din you could just make out the powerful *All Or Nothing* and *I Can Make It*.

After the interval it was time for the Searchers. The Merseybeat groups had now faded from the charts, but the Searchers were still a class act, with their catchy hits *Sugar And Spice*, *Needles And Pins* and *When You Walk In The Room*, though it was their version of Dylan's *Blowing In The Wind* that stopped the show that night. Reporter Steve Mann, who was covering the event for the *Aldershot News*, wrote, 'It almost succeeded in stopping the screams. In fact, it was one of the few numbers the audience really listened to in the whole show.'

Bill-topper Orbison, backed by the Candy Men, treated the Aldershot fans to a succession of hits, closing the show with *Only The Lonely*, *Lana*, *In Dreams* and *Pretty Woman*. The young and not so young gave him a standing ovation. He returned the compliment afterwards, thanking the fans for their generous reception. The tour had been tough and he was looking forward to a five-week break back home in the USA before getting back on the treadmill of recording and gigging.

Roy Orbison proudly displays this tribute to his hits, lovingly put together by a fan. (*Aldershot News*)

The teens eagerly gathered outside the cinema after the shows for a glimpse of the American idol. Among them was sixteen-year-old Aldershot mod David Paul, who has clear memories of the star:

He had a black suit on and his trademark dark glasses and winkelpickers. He came out of the side door and just made his way through to a big American car in the car park.

There were crowds there – boys and girls – calling out to him, shouting anything to get his attention. I was in amongst them, craning my head to get a view. This wasn't one or two people. It was more like a crowd of something over 100, maybe several hundred. Some of them had seen the show, but others, like me, hadn't been able to afford it and just turned up outside afterwards to get a glimpse of the stars. Roy Orbison got an excited reaction from the kids, but he didn't hang about. He was straight into the car and off.

The Small Faces, meanwhile, were bemoaning the state of the charts and the rise of the cosy ballad in favour of music with a more cutting edge. Reporter Mann asked Marriott what had happened to the group's latest single *I Can Make It*. 'Nothing,' came the reply. 'It didn't get the plugs as it was banned by the BBC for being too suggestive. It had advance orders of about 50,000, but hardly sold a copy after that.'

Did this worry him? 'No. I wouldn't worry if the whole scene folded up tomorrow. I'd concentrate more on songwriting, which gives me more pleasure than singing anyway.' And on the subject of those cosy ballads, Marriott remarked, 'Pop is going backwards. After all the Beatles have tried to do in pop music, a record like *Release Me* can keep them from the top of the charts. At this rate we'll probably see Vera Lynn back in the charts soon! It worries me, man.'

The tour was originally planned to reach Hammersmith Odeon the next night, but the date was cancelled at Orbison's request. He had been searching for an English nanny to look after his three young sons in the USA, but there had been a hitch in arranging a work permit and he requested that day off to go to the American Embassy to try to iron out the problems. At least it gave everyone a day off before the final night in Romford.

Orbison announced during the tour that he had no plans to return to the UK, but he was presented with a petition signed by more than 2,000 fans when the tour finished, pleading with him to change his mind.

How The Searchers got a look in...

While the Paul McCartneys of the pop world were zipping around London in their minis in the 1960s, the Searchers had to rely on more

Moody and magnificent... Searchers John Blunt, Frank Allen, Mike Pender and John McNally (foreground) in their dressing room. (*Aldershot News*)

traditional forms of transport. Founder member John McNally recalls: 'In the early days, none of us could drive. I got my first car in 1966 – a Cortina it was. I paid £649 for it – big money in those days – but I still couldn't drive even then.'

So when the Searchers stepped in to replace Paul and Barry Ryan for the last two dates on the Roy Orbison tour, it was down to the faithful old group van. John said:

We wouldn't have been on the tour bus for just two dates. The pictures from the Aldershot gig are great. There must be so many newspapers up and down the country with pictures like these in their files. Roy was just Roy, of course, professional and polished and with the dark glasses. It's hard to believe the place was only half full.

But he was quiet and kept himself to himself. We knew that from when we'd worked with him before.

The Searchers' bassist Frank Allen, who had taken over from Tony Jackson, recalled:

(Left) **Reporter Steve Mann takes notes while the Searchers hold court.** (*Aldershot News*)

(Right) **Searchers John McNally, left, and Frank Allen in their dressing room before a show at the Hexagon in Reading.** (Author's collection)

I remember that Roy's backing group, the Candy Men, were very much in the background. In fact, they sometimes played behind a gauze curtain, although you could still see them! John Blunt was our drummer then and he kicked his drums over at the end of our set at Aldershot and again on the last night.

It's funny how your mind plays tricks on you, though. I could have sworn that Paul and Barry Ryan played with us that night, but of course, they didn't, as we were replacing them!

Now I think about it, the other guys on the tour were telling me about their roadie playing bagpipes on stage with them and that nobody was allowed to take the piss out of them, or their roadie/minder would deal with them. While the groups would mess about during each other's act, no one did it while Paul and Barry were on because they were under Harold Davison's protection. He was married to their mother, singer Marion Ryan.

The Searchers made many friends on the tour buses but, like Herman's Hermits drummer Barry Whitwam, they recall the strictness of tour manager Fred Perry's timekeeping. If you were late, the bus went without you. Allen said:

The bus would start out from Alsop Place next to the London Planetarium. The Isley Brothers got left behind once. They all had to

The Searchers on stage at the Hexagon in Reading. (Author's collection)

jump in a cab, saying take us to Birmingham! Then came the inevitable debate about who was going to pay. But they were great days. We all mixed together. And yes, I remember the occasional séance too back at the hotels.

I can recall one from 1962 when I was with Cliff Bennett and the Rebel Rousers. Beryl Bryden was there. She played washboard on Lonnie Donegan's *Rock Island Line*. It was the Bruce Chanel tour, and Frank Ifield and Johnny Kidd were there too. I remember Frank taking part in the séance. We were backing him on that tour and he put in *I Remember You*. This was before it was released so nobody had heard it, but he wanted to try it out on live audiences. Of course, two months later he was huge.

McNally and Allen recalled the craziness of those tours:

Look at the Aldershot pictures with all the kids screaming – and the nurses all dancing at the front. Of course it was fun, but really the sound systems in those places – cinemas and the likes – were crap. They couldn't produce any decent sound and nobody could really hear much. It was just all about the excitement.

McNally noted that the Small Faces turned up that night in Aldershot:

They didn't always. If Steve Marriott fancied staying in the pub, or if there was something good on the telly, they wouldn't bother in those days. They were all bolshies. There were times we would have liked to have done the same, but you don't do that.

The Small Faces were finding their way then, but they didn't give a toss.

The Searchers, by contrast, certainly did care. Their reputation for reliability and professionalism had been hard earned and it is ironic that an early lapse had cost them a coveted place in the Brian Epstein stable. The group's strong melodies and sweet harmonies would certainly have appealed to the Epstein ear and the Searchers could provide melancholy along with the beat, but the story goes that Epstein saw them give a stumbling, drunken performance in the Cavern and passed up on the opportunity to sign them. By the time he realised how good they were, they had already fallen into the clutches of rival Tito Burns. 'It's a true story. That's just how it happened,' said McNally. 'We had all been drinking and our singer in those days, Johnny Sandon, was out of it. Brian saw us and wasn't at all impressed.'

That mistake was to cost them dear. Despite the Searchers' stunning chart successes from 1963–66, with six top five singles, including three number ones, they paid a heavy price:

We would have done 50 per cent better with Eppy. I firmly believe that. We were being worn to a frazzle by Tito Burns. We were knackered, totally drained. Tito was working us non stop because he thought it wouldn't last long – it would just be that generation – and he was right, in a way. He just wanted to make the most of it while he could, but it was no good for us. If we'd had any nouse we'd have told him to f*** off.

Epstein would have taken greater care of his artists, and, vitally, there would have been support from the Lennon and McCartney songbook. 'We'd have had access to the Beatles tunes. Other artists in the Epstein stable were given songs written by John and Paul, but of course we were working for someone else. It would have made a big difference. We were always scratching around for songs,' said McNally.

There was to be no big acrimonious split for the Searchers. They simply took themselves off the circuit for a while to recover from burnout. 'We were naïve about the business side of things. It was a silly mistake. We should have taken more notice of it. We left it to our drummer Chris Curtis, who retained the flat in London, and that wasn't really fair.'

Allen added:

The trouble was there were too many records and not enough thought between them. We did three LPs and four singles one year. It was too much, and you didn't get the studio time. They never wanted to fork out for it.

We felt we needed to get on with it. It wasn't legitimate to take months to make a record. Even if you had the power, you didn't feel it was right for you to do it. It was nothing for an A- and B-side to be recorded in a few hours, or for a whole album in a day.

before Eppy put them into suits. Harrison and Lennon running across the stage like Chuck Berry, and drinking and smoking on stage – acting the goat.

We weren't keen on the suits, but in the end we had to follow of course. That was the image and that's where the money was. Here we are, forty-odd years on, and people still associate us with the suits. We still wear them today.

When the story of the Searchers is finally told it will be an interesting read: highs and lows, pathos, betrayal, ecstasy and tragedy. It is all there waiting to be revealed.

The recent deaths of original drummer Chris Curtis and bassist Tony Jackson have left their mark on the survivors. The hurt is still raw, old feuds and words spoken in haste long forgotten. However, one dispute remains. McNally and fellow Searcher original Mike Pender have not spoken for more than twenty years after Pender quit to set up a rival band.

Despite this the Searchers are rocking on, still putting themselves in the firing line and still taking on sixty-plus gig UK tours, along with fellow Mersey mates such as the Swinging Blue Jeans, Gerry and the Pacemakers and the Merseybeats.

It is not just UK fans who enjoy the group. They were booked for a six-week stint in New Zealand and Australia at the start of 2007, having already rocked New York and other American cities in 2006. At least the old group van and tour buses have been consigned to history.

The coalman's mate who became a star

John Blunt, the Searchers drummer when they joined the Roy Orbison tour, laughed as he recalled his grand finale:

Oh yeah, it was true about me kicking the drums over. I used to do that. I was a Who fanatic and people said I used to copy Keith Moon, and I did.

I'd go into my solo and then it would end up with me kicking seven bells out of the kit. Some people said it wasn't right, a Searchers drummer doing that kind of thing, but the lads didn't seem to mind and it was left in the act. The crowd would get into the spirit of it too and there were a lot of laughs.

Blunt was a raw eighteen year old then and confesses that although he was with the stars under the bright lights on stage, he was sharing the excitement of the youngsters shouting themselves hoarse from the audience:

And of course, you didn't get the rewards. We were on royalties of between 2 per cent and 4 per cent. It was ridiculous. Later, people were getting 25 per cent, or better still publishing their own stuff. But we didn't understand the business side of it.

The Searchers had played with the Beatles at countless Merseyside gigs in the early pre-record contract days, but as a Tito Burns act the group never got to tour with their old mates. It did not stop them being Beatle fans, McNally recalled:

We first played alongside them at St John's Hall in Liverpool. They were the Silver Beatles then and they got £6.50 and we got £4.50. Dave Forshaw was the promoter.

To me, the Beatles were the best rock 'n' roll band ever. People talk about the Rolling Stones, but they couldn't put a penny to the Beatles. The Beatles did it first and they did it better. I always remember the leather jacketed Beatles at the Cavern and the Star Club in Hamburg

I was in my element on that 1967 Roy Orbison package, because the Small Faces were on it and they were my idols. I was like a fan really and I would make sure I was around to watch them coming in. I idolised these guys we were touring with – Roy Orbison and Steve Marriott. Steve had such a great voice. Steve and the other Faces would arrive long after we did. We used to get there quite early, but they would get there maybe 20 minutes or half an hour before the show. They would all be in their Daimler and I knew that Steve had a lot of girls in that back seat!

The Searcher was thrilled when Marriott turned to him for some help. 'Steve was tinkering around on the drums in the break and I showed him a couple of things. Here I was passing on a few tips to my idol. I was only eighteen and the Small Faces were such a big name on the mod circuit, and I was a mod.'

He was also pleased to spend some time with Roy Orbison: 'He was very friendly. We had a chat at the side of the stage for 4 or 5 minutes

(Left) **The Merseybeat boom was over, but the Searchers were still a quality band as the youngsters at the ABC Cinema in Aldershot discovered over the screams.** *(Aldershot News)*

(Right) **Former Searchers drummer John Blunt, pictured in 2006 by the author.**

one night. I asked him what he thought of audiences here and he said they were very responsive and how much he enjoyed being in England. He was still getting great receptions – all the screaming.'

And what did it feel like to be on stage that night in Aldershot?

The girlfriend I had at the time said that when I launched into a drum solo the girls were screaming like mad but I couldn't hear them. You couldn't really hear the audience much in those big places.

It's funny, because when you stood at the side of the stage you could hear more, and see it all, but when you were actually out there with the lights on you, you didn't. Being back line, the drummer, I didn't really hear a lot of what was going on. I could see now and again the kids running around, trying to get to the stage and the bouncers keeping them back, but I couldn't really hear. It was inaudible.

The set we played was only about 20 minutes – half an hour. That was it – end of! Eight numbers and finish. There was lots of hanging around. You couldn't always go out because you'd get your clothes ripped.

The waiting about was one of the negative aspects of touring. John remembers:

It seemed like you spent 80 per cent of the time just hanging around. I remember Charlie Watts complaining about it, and he was right. You

van, hotel, dressing room – it was just ridiculous. Mike Pender said to me 'you'd shag anything, you would' … and I would.

And the drugs?

I was involved in some of it, mainly the soft stuff, but yeah, I was part of that family. I was always partying, always at it, especially drink-wise. In those days it was all about what we used to call the happy pills, Purple Hearts. Sometimes we'd be up all night dancing and then feeling like shit the next day. But that's the way it was. I was that kind of guy. They were quite straight, though, the Searchers. They didn't do the drugs and they didn't drink very much, whereas I was always drinking. I didn't do drugs on the road, but if we did a week's cabaret, I used to be behind with the girls, drinking. All those Bunny Girls were very nice people, you know!

Life as a Searcher had begun a few months before, in the spring of 1966. Blunt's first gig was at Birmingham Town Hall on the P.J. Proby tour. It proved memorable:

The drummer in Proby's band was drunk. Another band on the tour were called Ace and I was stood watching with their drummer. Proby's drummer started swaying and the guy eventually fell off his stool. The drummer from Ace had to take over – there was no way I was going to! Then later on a girl fell off the balcony and split her head open on the Hammond organ – so that was my debut gig with the Searchers!

Our roadie back then, Barry Delaney, went on to become a Labour MP – another great character and a friend of Frank's. He was with us for about two years, so he was still there for the Orbison tour.

Proby was quite a character – but quite an angry person at times. I remember there was a promotional cardboard cut-out of him at this town hall. He came out for the second of the two shows and it was only about half full. He kicked this cut-out all round the stage, saying that's what he wanted to do to his manager or the promoter.

Becoming a Searcher was not straightforward. Blunt's girlfriend had found out, through a friend's father, that Chris Curtis might be leaving and Blunt, who was a coalman's mate at the time, secured an audition. He was to meet an agent at 3 p.m. in Regent Street to be taken to the audition:

Well this coalman said Can I come with you? And I said Yeah, I don't mind. So we got the round done quick, parked the lorry up and both rushed home and put our suits on. We went up on the train to Regent Street to go to the Harold Davison agency office to meet the Searchers. This coalman was a real street-wise geezer – braces on, the lot – and they must have thought Who the hell are these two guys? We got in this taxi to take us to a studio for the audition. So we're sitting there like a couple of punters, facing John and Mike, and this coalman said

couldn't get out or anything, with all the screaming kids. That's what it was like – and all for 20 minutes on stage.

So much emotion on the faces of the fans. (*Aldershot News*)

However, Blunt found ways to pass the time. The other Searchers were settled down – John McNally and Mike Pender were newlyweds – but Blunt was an eighteen year old ready to party. For him, it was sex and drugs and rock 'n' roll – with bucket-loads of booze thrown in:

We only had the one roadie and the one van in those days. I've got photos of it still with all the lipstick all over it, with messages like I love John or Frank. Oh those days. They were funny days. The van was always covered in so much muck – pencil liner and lipstick. It was part of it all. It was fun, you know. How I never caught a dose I don't know to this day! When I joined them, the two original guys had not long been married and they were loyal to their wives. But I was like a rabbit all those years I was with them. First of all it was younger girls – but then slightly older when we moved into cabaret – back of the

There was time for the odd press interview on tour. *Aldershot News* reporter Steve Mann is taking the notes. (*Aldershot News*)

You lot, you've been on the Palladium haven't you? And Frank said yes, we have. I think about it now and cringe. The impression those guys must have had.

Things went quiet after the audition and the agent arranged for Blunt to meet a Dutch band. Then the phone call came, with the message: 'Get your passport, you're going to Rome for a TV appearance with the Searchers!' 'We did the TV show in Rome and we got back. A couple of days later he phoned me and said yes, you're definitely on the P.J. Proby tour a week or so later, and that was it. That was the beginning. I couldn't believe my luck.'

Even then, Blunt was not convinced he was in the band for good – until he came face to face with *Ready Steady Go*'s Cathy McGowan live on television:

She turned to me and said 'What's it like to be the drummer of the Searchers?' I said I didn't know I was, and then she said to Frank Allen 'Where did you find him?' And he said under a gooseberry bush. There were a couple of other light-hearted remarks. I was elated I'd got the job because they auditioned another guy in the Fiesta Club, Stockton, while I was on the road with them. He was a better drummer than me, but they reckoned he didn't look right. They weren't sure what to do but Barry said give Johnny the gig – he's a lot prettier than the other geezer anyway! And Frank said Yeah, give him the gig, and they did.

I was nearly four years with them and I count my blessings. I was lucky to get that break. I could have used it better, but I was young – I liked my drink – big time – and that didn't help me.

I got on well with the other Searchers, but I was younger than them, and really I was a young teenager. They were a lot older, not just in years, but mentally. They'd had a lot of problems with Tito Burns and a lot of financial things. We split company with Tito around 1967/68, and Tony Hatch went too. So suddenly we were on our own and didn't have any set producer until we got Kenny Young, who produced us under the name Pasha. I know they had meetings and they were quite angry at times. I didn't go to them. I kept out of it because really I just drummed for them. I wasn't asked to go to those sort of meetings and I wouldn't have wanted to. But they were lucky to have Frank Allen. He's got a good brain, Frank. He's quite an academic sort of geezer. He was good for them, not just on stage as a frontman. He was quite shrewd and astute and I used to look up to him a lot. They are nice people, the Searchers.

Along with the UK tours and foreign trips, there were two gigs in the Cavern Club in Mathew Street, Liverpool, where the Searchers had cut their musical teeth, along with the Beatles. Sadly, John was too young to fully appreciate the history of the place:

Quite frankly, I didn't like it. The acoustics were shit. You banged the drum and it sounded like a canon going off. It would have meant more to me today, but of course it doesn't exist now – there's only a reproduced Cavern built near where the original one was. It was ridiculous, what that council did. Fancy, filling that in. The history of that place, but that's councils for you.

Perhaps surprisingly for a drummer who enjoyed beating hell out of his kit, John was quite at home on the cabaret circuit. 'I enjoyed the cabaret because everything was all worked out very nicely and I used to really get off on the actual show. I really did enjoy it, especially Pender. It's sad that he left.'

One of the best things about being a Searcher was who you got to rub shoulders with. Right there at the very top for John was Jimi Hendrix, and being a drummer, John got to know his Experience counterpart Mitch Mitchell better than the others:

I was a big fan. Jimi's ability with electrics alone was awesome. He used every effect to its maximum, wah-wah, chorus pedal, you name it. I still listen to his early stuff. To me, he was the instigator when it came to electric guitars.

Mitch joined the Experience when it was formed in March 1966, at about the time I was joining the Searchers. I got to know Mitch and Noel Redding the bass player. Noel was a very angry guy. The last time I met him was at the club above the Marquee in Wardour Street. It was around this time that Hendrix split the band and what Noel was calling Hendrix, I wouldn't repeat. He was slagging him down rotten. Apparently, it was quite well known that there was a lot of bitching going on between him and Hendrix. I don't know if it was because he was coaxed into playing bass, because he was a lead guitarist.

John also clearly remembers his first meeting with Hendrix, after an Experience gig:

It was at the Star Hotel, Croydon, which had originally been called the Crawdaddy Club. I had just bought this Jag, being the flash mod that I was. I had only just turned nineteen and I was always getting pulled over by the police.

I went to get in the car that night and the police came over, and while they were questioning me, Hendrix came out with the other two and another guy who was driving this beaten up yellow Ford Escort. Jimi said 'Them pigs giving you trouble man?'

I had never heard that expression before – pigs – and I was quite pleased he said it because I thought – you spoke to me! Because I'd just loved that guy's playing that night. *Hey Joe* was zooming up the charts and it was amazing that they played these little pubs.

Blunt is still a working musician today, although he now sings and plays guitar. He would be happy to meet his old Searchers mates if their paths cross again:

Folksters the Settlers – John Fyffe, Cindy Kent and Mike Jones – hold their own at the Aldershot ABC. (*Aldershot News*)

I left the Searchers at the end of 1969, beginning of 1970. I would like to see them again and have a chat with them, because it has been such a long time. The last time I saw them was at Fairfield Halls in Croydon. John McNally said to me that night that if I'd joined them a year or two later he thinks I'd still be with them. And I said, well you may be right. I was a very young teenager, but I've grown up a bit now!

Blunt's drum kit from his Searcher days is now gathering dust on the memorabilia shelf of the Rock Bottom music shop in Croydon. However, he is proud that his son James is following in his footsteps – he is the drummer of the Fore.

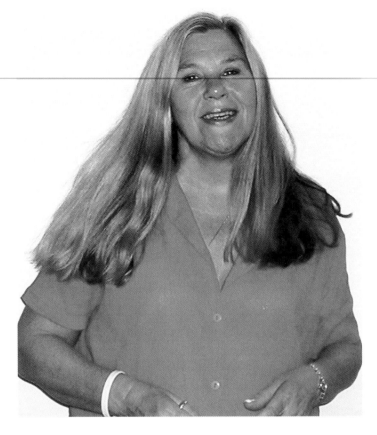

Former Settlers singer Cindy Kent pictured by the author one afternoon in August 2005 before her Premier Radio show.

Settler Cindy and a highly strung Big O

Settlers singer Cindy Kent has rather mixed memories of that eventful opening night of the Roy Orbison tour.

On the down side, there was the anguish of the group having their money stolen from their dressing room at the Finsbury Park Astoria while they were performing. However, a gallant Steve Marriott rode to the rescue by quickly organising a whip-round to make sure they were not out of pocket. 'I'll never forget his kindness,' said Cindy, who now hosts a regular afternoon show on Premier Radio in Pimlico, London.

The thing is, we didn't have much money and the cash that was stolen was meant to pay for our digs and tour expenses. I can't remember how much it was, but it was a lot to us.

Backstage at the Astoria was like a rabbit warren, with numerous stairways. Someone must have just sneaked in. As soon as Steve heard what had happened, he organised the collection from the other performers. It was very sweet of him and it saved the day for us.

They may have had a hard rock 'n' roll reputation, but the Small Faces were all great guys. P.P. Arnold and I were the only girls on the tour, so we shared a dressing room, and the boys were always very good to us, although I occasionally had to block my ears on the bus with some of the language flying around.

The Settlers were also good to the Small Faces' drummer Kenney Jones. They provided a haven of sanity in their dressing room for Kenny to practise the odd spot of drumming when the chaos of the Faces' dressing room got too much.

There was another reason to smile at the end of that opening show – when Jonathan King and Walker Brother Scott Engel came into the Settlers' dressing room to congratulate them. 'Jonathan came rushing

over and said we were great,' said Cindy. 'It was a nice boost, especially in light of our money being stolen.'

The trio were originally a duo – banjo player John Fyffe and guitarist Mike Jones – playing the folk clubs around Birmingham. Singer Cindy spotted them one night and they were soon heading for the bright lights of London.

The tour gave the Settlers a chance to showcase their new single – a cover version of Lennon and McCartney's *Nowhere Man*. The fact that they were not screamable idols meant the kids would hear their songs on this tour. Cindy said:

They appreciated us. We could play our numbers and they would be listening, and at the end they would applaud. It was the same with Roy, of course. His fans wanted to hear him play and they didn't scream over him.

That was the beauty of putting tour packages together like this – the Small Faces and Paul and Barry Ryan – and then Roy and us.

The funny thing about us was that we could play a folk club one night and go down well, and we could also play at a pop show in front of hundreds of teenagers and go down well.

The Orbison tour was typical, with bands happy to mix in together. 'There was always so much chatter going on – on the tour bus and at the venues and digs. Nothing was out of bounds – sex, drugs, politics, religion – we chewed the fat about it all,' said Cindy.

If the first night was memorable, so was the last, in Romford on Sunday 9 April. Final night equalled prank night and it was normally the star who copped it. Roy '*Only The Lonely*' Orbison was very much a loner on these tours. He had certainly not been chewing the fat about the state of the world. Withdrawn he may have been, but none of his compatriots mistook that for unfriendliness and, mercifully, he had a good sense of humour. Cindy recalls:

Roy would come down on stage during the interval while the curtain was closed and tune his guitar. His stool would be beside it. But on the last night his band came down after, and I think it was the pianist who retuned Roy's guitar a whole tone higher. And Roy sang very high anyway! So the curtains opened and the announcer said Ladies and Gentleman please put your hands together for the one and only Roy Orbison and he was perched on his stool and as soon as he began strumming he immediately realised what they had done. Of course, he had to carry on.

We were in the wings laughing for all we were worth, but of course the audience were none the wiser and his backing band were just looking down at their dots and keeping their heads down. He said Nice one, guys, and of course they played everything in lower keys after that to compensate.

It was typical of what would go on during a final night and he took it very well. Roy was quiet – I had maybe two dozen words with him during the whole tour. But he was a loner. It was just the way he was.

Cindy recalled another tour when she was the last night victim:

It happened when I was on tour with Alan Price's band and Dusty Springfield. I had got right to the end of the final number and was building up for the big finish when two members of Alan's band came on, grabbed me, and carried me horizontally off the stage while I was still singing. Goodness knows what the audience made of that!

Cindy recalled Dusty on tour:

Poor thing, she was as blind as a bat. I can still see her half an inch from the mirror trying to put her make-up on. And she would head somewhere quiet like a fire escape gargling with Port and practising her scales. And what a voice she had. What a talent. She was complimentary about us too. We saw ourselves as a latterday Springfields.

The Settlers got their big break on a Monday night television series in Scotland called *Singalong*. It featured folk acts and was supposed to last six weeks, but ended up running for six months, and the Settlers

A moment or two for quiet man Roy Orbison to relax. (*Aldershot News*)

appeared every Monday. They quickly decided it was time to turn professional.

The guests one week were the Seekers who had headed over from Australia to take our charts by storm. The two groups became friendly and still are. Singer Judith Durham invited Cindy to her sixtieth birthday party in London in 2004 and Cindy did a live link-up with Seeker Keith Potger in Australia to plug his album on Premier Radio in 2005.

Cindy recalled them playing a new song to her off air before a *Singalong* show:

Judith just casually said would you like to hear this song we recorded today that Tom Springfield has written for us? They then sang *I'll Never Find Another You* and I knew instantly that it would be huge. What we would have done for a song like that.

Sometimes, that's what it takes – one really great song. But of course it was more than that with the Seekers. They had lots of talent and we got on really well. Our bass players even looked alike and I played a tambourine – as Judith did for the Seekers!

The Searchers only joined the Roy Orbison tour for the final two dates, but it was enough to make an impact on Cindy and the other Settlers:

They were a very nice bunch and they were talented too,' said Cindy. 'I can remember one funny thing, though, when our two groups were on the TV show *Thank Your Lucky Stars*. The Searchers bass guitarist Frank Allen had got held up flying back from somewhere on holiday and so they filmed them in silhouette with one of our guitarists, Mike Jones, standing in for him ... and nobody noticed!

Note perfect... Cinema staff reported that Roy Orbison sounded just as good live as he did on record. (*Aldershot News*)

Tickets for the big shows earned me brownie points!

Mod Brian Coxhill was earning £4 a week as a seventeen-year-old trainee mechanic at Solomons garage in Camberley in April 1967, so he did not have money to throw around. He did, however, have his pride and joy, a Lambretta LI 150, and a determination to impress a girl called Diane, with whom he had just started going out, and what better way than by buying two tickets for a pop show and taking her there on the back of his scooter?

Diane was a lucky girl. Not only did she get to see the Roy Orbison show on 7 April, but she was also there to witness the Walker Brothers three weeks later.

Brian, who has lived in the nearby town of Yateley all his life, recalled:

How privileged I felt to be able to see all these wonderful stars. To see all those bands on the same show for just a few shillings – I couldn't believe my luck. It felt like I'd died and gone to heaven. Looking back, we were in the right place at the right time. It was like a music explosion in the 1960s.

Brian, who like many mods enjoyed Motown and soul sounds, was impressed by the line-up, but it was not the music that made him buy the tickets. 'The primary objective was to impress Diane and I guess it worked because we went out for a while.'

On the first show, was Roy Orbison. Brian remembered:

He sang *Pretty Woman* and *Only The Lonely* and I thought, fantastic, this is Roy Orbison. There were so many people there to pay homage to their icons and I couldn't believe I was lucky enough to be part of it. The lads didn't join in the screaming and shouting. For us, it was just about showing respect. Roy was a good performer.

The Settlers made an impression, too: 'I still remember them singing the Beatles' song, *Nowhere Man*. I liked that song and the girl singer had a nice voice,' he said.

The show three weeks later had an even more impressive line-up:

We were sitting downstairs on the right hand side about halfway down for the Walker Brothers show. We had a really good view, until, that is, the Walkers

came on and the girls were standing on the seats waving their scarves.

I'd have to put my feet under the back of the seats of the girls in front to tip them off so we could see! They were particularly excited about Scott.

Diane also got caught up in the excitement. Brian said:

She was hysterical for the Walkers, joining in all that screaming. They sang *My Ship Is Coming In*, but I enjoyed Cat Stevens – I recall him wearing a sage green coat and a cowboy hat to sing *I'm Gonna Get Me A Gun*. He looked quite trendy.

Jimi Hendrix made quite an impact:

I'd never seen anyone play the guitar like that. It was such revolutionary music – so vibrant – and for a country boy like me, it felt like we'd hit the big time just to be there.

Brian looks back fondly on the period. The Lambretta was his passport to the mod world.

We used to go around – about a dozen of us – a big crowd of old school friends. We were all sixteen or seventeen – just old enough to have some mechanical transport – and our Lambrettas were our freedom to get around.

Smart young mod Brian Coxhill in the 1960s.
(Courtesy of Brian Coxhill)

Brian Coxhill in 2006.
(Author's collection)

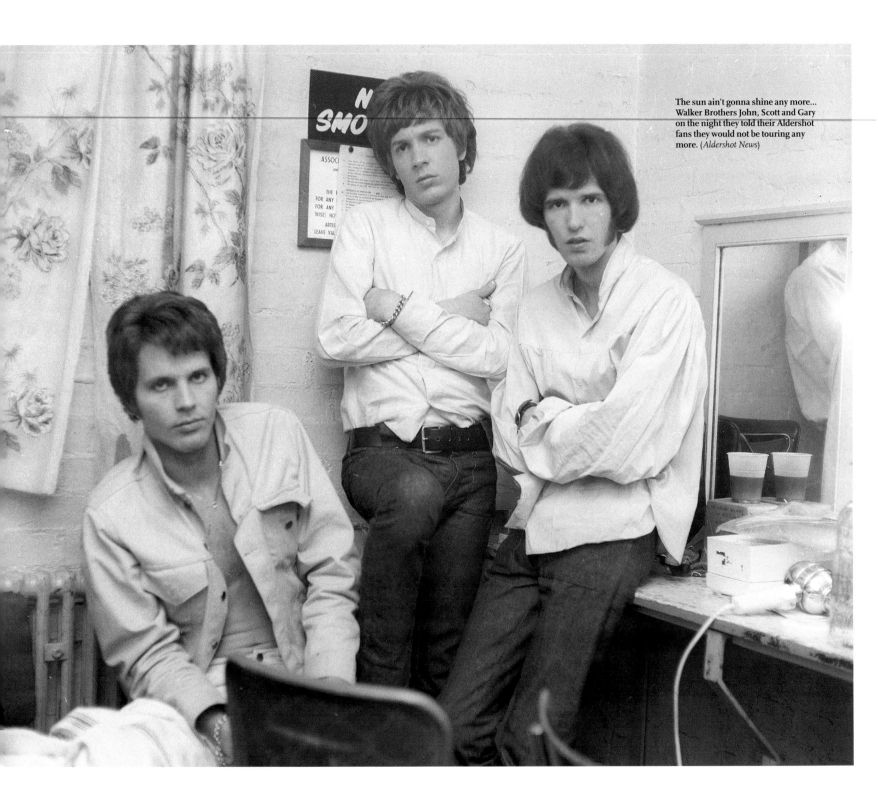

The sun ain't gonna shine any more... Walker Brothers John, Scott and Gary on the night they told their Aldershot fans they would not be touring any more. (*Aldershot News*)

Seven

The Walkers, Jimi, Cat and Engelbert Tour

Getting ready to rumble

IT WAS THE pop tour to top them all, featuring four of the biggest and most diverse names in the music world. Rubbing shoulders for a month on the twenty-five-gig UK tour in April 1967 were Engelbert Humperdinck for the ladies, Cat Stevens for the cool cats, Jimi Hendrix for the ravers and, topping the bill, heart-throbs the Walker Brothers.

The tour, promoted by the Walkers' manager Maurice King and impressario Tito Burns, was evolving by the week when it was announced at the beginning of the year. The Move were part of the original plans, but pulled out. However, other big names were being added as the start date neared.

First on board was Cat Stevens who was announced at the end of January, quickly followed by Hendrix the week after and Engelbert just before the dates were finally announced.

Then came the mad scramble for tickets. The tour was to open at the Finsbury Park Astoria, London, on Friday 31 March, and end back in London at the Tooting Granada on 30 April, and towns up and down the country wondered exactly what would happen when this most unusual collection of musical talent descended on them.

After the opening night, the Odeon cinemas at Ipswich, Worcester, Leeds, and Glasgow were next on the list, followed by the ABC cinemas at Carlisle and Chesterfield, on 7 and 8 April, and the Liverpool Empire on 9 April. The Bedford Granada would have its moment on 11 April and then the Southampton public could consider themselves fortunate to get their piece of the action when the town's Gaumont was host to the two shows on 12 April after the Kingsway Theatre at Hadleigh in Essex had rather hastily cancelled due to poor ticket sales a few weeks before for the Orbison package.

The Walkers tour poster from the Southampton Gaumont in 1967. Note the misspelling of Engelbert. (Courtesy of the Mayflower Theatre, Southampton, and Engelbert Humperdinck)

Next stops were the Gaumont Cinema in Wolverhampton and the Odeons at Bolton and Blackpool before hitting Engelbert's home town of Leicester at the De Montfort Hall on 16 April.

After a three-day break the tour would resume at the Odeon Birmingham, before moving on swiftly to the ABC Lincoln, Newcastle City Hall, Odeon Manchester and the Gaumont at Hanley. Then there was the Colston Hall, Bristol, a brief stop in Wales at the Cardiff Capitol on 26 April, before moving on to Aldershot the next night. The tour would then be set for the last few dates at the Slough Adelphi and the Winter Gardens at Bournemouth before the final show in Tooting.

There was plenty of apprehension in the days running up to the tour as each artist wondered what sort of reception they would get from fans of the others. The Walker Brothers had the easiest job, as up to 90 per cent of audiences would be teenage girls who had come to see them; however, it was the Walkers who had the least enthusiasm. The group was to famously announce it was splitting just days after the tour finished.

Scott Engel gave a hint of what was to come in a hard hitting pre-tour interview. He said pop tours would be dead within a year and this would be the Walker Brothers' last – he was right on both counts:

It isn't that we don't like touring, but we don't want to be part of a dying scene, and the pop tour as it stands today is a dying scene.

Although our box office figures are the best ever – but that may be because of the strength of the supporting artists – you can get a pointer of the way things are going by seeing who people are bringing in to tour. People like Tony Bennett and Count Basie.

He was predicting that the group would perhaps go into television with a Monkees-style music series, or (say it quietly) the dreaded cabaret.

The Walkers had put together a large backing band for a fuller sound and were promising to bounce around on stage.

Scott was complimentary about his tour colleagues, describing Cat Stevens as 'a great recording talent' and praising Hendrix similarly. Engelbert received the highest praise. About him Scott said, 'I sincerely consider him to be the biggest new talent to be discovered in Britain. For a change, here's a man with real professional polish and subtlety to his voice. Lovely delivery.'

This was quite a shot in the arm for Engelbert who was under fire from many quarters for daring to be the first artist for four years to keep the Beatles off the number one spot. Worse still, the Fabs' double A-side *Penny Lane/Strawberry Fields* was considered possibly their best work, and Engelbert had pipped them with *Release Me*, known for its family appeal.

Release Me sales were approaching the million mark running up to the tour and Engelbert was answering his critics with a modest charm offensive. He said:

Engelbert reaches out to a besotted fan on his November tour, in a picture which featured boldly in that week's edition of the *Aldershot News*. (*Aldershot News*)

I'm not going to brag about beating the Beatles. They are, after all, so big that they don't need me as competition. I thought their material on the new single was first class. In fact, I was one of the first people to go out and buy *Penny Lane*. It's quite one of the best records they've done. How they get their ideas I do not know. I'd love to have just a tiny piece of their genius for writing.

Being kept out of the number one spot won't affect them in the slightest. The Beatles will never start going downhill.

Engelbert was in an equally generous mood when asked if he would steal the show ahead of the other big names. He replied to this:

I'm really a nobody yet compared with the Walker Brothers, who are monster names. I'm really excited about this tour, though. I shall have a four-piece backing group. They haven't got a name and if anybody has any ideas I'd be interested to hear them. Anyway, I won't be doing just ballads. There'll be beat as well.

The bill does look a bit mixed. Still, it should give everybody a piece of everything. I've only seen the Walkers once, but the impression they left was outstanding.

Cat Stevens and Jimi Hendrix were as yet a mystery to him. 'I don't know much about them,' Engelbert confessed, 'but I'm looking forward to seeing them. I always like watching the rest of a show from the wings.'

Cat, meanwhile, was holed-up getting ready for the tour. Acknowledged as a promising songwriter, he had, however, attracted some criticism for the rawness of his live performances. 'I'm working very hard on a stage act,' he said. Referring to his performance at the Saville Theatre Christmas Show a few months before, he said: 'I was just bunged into the show on the strength of a couple of hits. I should have waited, but still, people got to know me. As long as I can write forever, that's great, but I don't want to sing forever.'

As the tour drew near, Cat was helped by his latest single, *I'm Gonna Get Me A Gun*, racing up the charts. Even that drew a defensive response. 'By the word "gun" I am not condoning violence,' he said. 'It's a song about someone who's been demoralised too many times, but now he's coming back with a bang.'

He was also hoping to get his personality over on the tour:

I like signing autographs for people. I like to act like ordinary Steve Adams [his real name]. I've noticed that people who come up to me are dubious of talking to me because they think I've become big-headed. This is really not true. I want to be so friendly, and instead this is the image that has come up about me.

The person most justified in approaching the tour with trepidation was the outstanding new talent, Jimi Hendrix. Hendrix had exploded onto the London scene just three months before with an amazing performance at the new mecca, the Bag O' Nails Club, where a star-studded audience had been on its feet paying homage to the new king. Beatles Paul and Ringo, together with manager Brian Epstein, Rolling Stone Bill Wyman, Who guitarist Pete Townshend, Hollies Bobby Elliott and Allan Clarke, plus Eric Clapton, Lulu, Donovan, Denny Laine, Eric Burdon and Georgie Fame were among those dazzled by this new phenomenon.

Jimi was the protégé of Animals bassist Bryan 'Chas' Chandler and it was Chandler who persuaded Hendrix to try his luck in the UK. Chas had spotted Hendrix strutting his stuff in a Greenwich Village coffee bar in New York, and his timing was perfect. Hendrix, who had earned a fine reputation backing stars such as Little Richard, was tiring of playing a supporting role. However, this first UK tour could make or break Jimi and the Experience. What if British audiences were not ready for their particular brand of mayhem? Just what would the Walkers' teeny-bopper fans make of them? Hendrix himself was quick to voice his fears:

It's effortless for Engelbert. (*Aldershot News*)

I'm a bit worried about the type of people who're gonna see the tour, If they come to see the Walker Brothers then they're not going to want us. I just hope they listen, but if they do scream for the Walkers during our act I'll just ignore them and play for myself.

The band were confident of their ability, but how would they cope in adverse circumstances? Hendrix concluded:

I dig the kind of people who come to hear us very much, but some of the places on the tour we only play once so maybe we won't get as much support as we'd like. And man, we need help from the people who know us.

could hardly be blamed for not understanding his music, but the man who was to go down as among the most important rock stars ever to strap on a guitar went through his whole repertoire of brilliance in front of a bemused and underwhelmed young audience.

His set consisted of four numbers, *Foxy Lady*, *Can You See Me* and his two hits, *Hey Joe* and *Purple Haze*. If the gamble didn't immediately pay off, Hendrix merely shrugged his shoulders. 'We did wonder how they would accept us,' he admitted afterwards, 'there being so many different acts and us probably the most extreme of all.'

It was certainly an extreme finish. Hendrix set his guitar alight, much to the discomfort of Walker Brothers' media man Brian Somerville and compère Nicky Jones who burned their hands trying to stop it setting the curtains alight, with Jones also suffering the contents of a fire extinguisher in his face. Hendrix simply strolled off the stage.

His explanation was not too convincing. 'I was on my knees at the time and the guitar had kept giving me slight electric shocks and shorting out. When it burst into flames I was kinda shocked and that's why I just ran off.'

This was complete bunkum; the stunt had been thought up in the dressing room, with a roadie dispatched to get lighter fuel. The burning of the guitar was to become an occasional ritual and Hendrix finished his spot at the three-day Monterey Festival on the west coast of America just a few weeks later with another bout of pyrotechnics.

By amazing contrast, as Jimi left the stage, it was time for Engelbert to take over to close the first half. And what a contrast it was!

As the ultimate rock 'n' roll rebel exited, so entered the man with the velvet voice dressed in his dapper tux: every inch a smooth entertainer.

Humperdinck, with his big voice his big asset, certainly held his own on that opening night. He kicked in with *Ain't That Good News*, *Yours Until Tomorrow*, *Midnight Hour*, *Let Me Be Yours*, *Ten Guitars* and *Jambalaya*, displaying the depth of his vocal talent, but it was the classic *Summertime* and his big hit *Release Me* that really got the crowd in a spin.

Afterwards, caught up in the excitement of it all, he proclaimed, 'Gerry Dorsey is dead. Now it is Engelbert Humperdinck forever. A name like that only comes once in a blue moon. I happened to catch that moon. Gerry Dorsey just doesn't exist any more.'

The Quotations opened the second half, before Cat Stevens, in a green Edwardian frock coat, strolled into the limelight.

Cat was reaping the rewards of all that time tucked away polishing up his performance. The nervous, awkward performer of three months ago had been replaced by the cool Cat who tripped off the Tremeloes hit *Here Comes My Baby* with ease from his stool, followed by his own rising chartbuster *I'm Gonna Get Me A Gun*. The stetson and gunbelt he wore added to the drama. He also threw in *Matthew And Son*, which was just slipping out of the charts after ten weeks during which time it had peaked at number two, plus *I Love My Dog* and *If I Were A Carpenter*.

'Obscene' ... but heard!

The Californians get the party going on the Walkers 1967 tour. (*Aldershot News*)

The first night, at an overexcited Astoria in Finsbury Park, went according to form. The girls screamed and screamed for the Walkers, and then screamed some more.

Scott was still giving out pessimistic interviews, but all the doom and gloom was lost on the girls. The music press carried photos of the hysteria, with one girl pictured trying to vault over the orchestra pit, while others carried on screaming regardless.

First up were the Quotations, who also had a small spot in the second half and were kept busy backing Cat Stevens and the Walkers. Compère Nick Jones then came on to introduce the Californians and finally it was the turn of the first of the big guns, the Jimi Hendrix Experience.

For the moment, Jimi's fears were confirmed as he battled on through a fairly lukewarm reception on that opening night. The teens

Then it was time for the embattled compère to introduce the act the girls had all been waiting for, amid the predictable wall of screams.

The Walkers, entering from separate sides of the stage – Scott in black, with a white smock, and John in a royal blue frock coat and white Levis – kicked off with *Land of A Thousand Dances* and they never looked back.

Hold On I'm Coming was followed by *What Now My Love?* as the stage lights flashed and the girls wept. *The Sun Ain't Gonna Shine Any More* was next and then *I Need You* before John took over with *Let Me Hear You Say Yeh*. Scott was soon back centre stage for *Livin' Above Your Head*. There was also time for drummer Gary to enjoy his solo spot with *Turn On Your Light* before they finished on a high with *Oop Oop A Doop*.

What an opening night: non-stop screams from the fans and positive reviews by the critics. It was meat and drink to Engelbert, Cat and the Walkers whose music sat nicely with the teenage girls who made up around 95 per cent of the audience. But what would fate have in store for Jimi? His explosive finish had not been enough to win over the teenies. No matter, Jimi was already a real trouper and it was on to Ipswich the next night and Worcester the night after that. The show was now truly on the road.

Jimi was famed for his amazing stage antics: playing the guitar with his teeth, behind the back of his neck, and even in a sexually suggestive way. These amazing pieces of skill and showmanship were condemned as obscene during the tour and pressure was put on him to cut them out.

As the show got into its second week, tour manager Don Finlayson apparently attempted to read him the riot act, with threats that he would be dropped. In true rock 'n' roll rebel tradition, however, Hendrix was having none of it. He told a music reporter:

The tour manager told me to stop using all this in my act because he said it was obscene and vulgar. I have been threatened every night of the tour so far and I'm not going to stop for him.

There's nothing vulgar about it at all. I've been using this act all the way since I've been in Britain. I just don't know where these people get the idea from that it's an obscene act.

There remains a probability that these arguments were exaggerated to cement Hendrix's wild man image, but in any event there were other setbacks. Hendrix ended up with stitches in a foot – injured by a broken fuzz-box at Chesterfield on 8 April – but he gamely battled on through the second house. Although, he need not have bothered as far as some of the mums and dads who had come to see Engelbert were concerned: a number just upped and walked out as Jimi closed the first half.

He fared little better at Birmingham and even reduced his second set at Bolton to three numbers after they blanked him there during the first house, so take a bow the people of Carlisle who reportedly

Cat Stevens has the audience in the palm of his hand. (*Aldershot News*)

gave Hendrix a rousing reception at their town's ABC Cinema. A full house of 2,000 screamed through the Experience set with St John Ambulance staff reviving hysterical girls and only *Purple Haze* able to be made out above the din. This was one night when even compère Nicky Jones was drowned out by Hendrix fans as he attempted to herald the entrance of Engelbert.

The Californians were struggling for attention in such illustrious company but they got a rousing reception from their home fans when the tour reached the Wolverhampton Gaumont on Thursday 13 April. Their Beach Boyish harmonies earned them big applause as the crowd waited for the big names. Hendrix was on ripping form, but his class was still largely lost on the teen multitude.

The Gaumont developed a new tactic to deal with the hysteria, and it worked perfectly. The new rule was that any fainting girl, once revived, would under no circumstances be allowed back in for the rest of the show. A total of twenty girls had fainted at the previous show, but this night, despite all the excitement, only one girl succumbed. 'These girls

Take it easy, Cat, they're fans, not critics! (*Aldershot News*)

Reporter Steve Mann joins teenager Janice Parsonage for a tête-à-tête with the Jimi Hendrix Experience. (*Aldershot News*)

are only exhibitionists,' said manager Joe Alexander afterwards. 'Once they know they won't see any more when they faint, they manage, somehow, to restrain themselves.'

How other venues could have done with Mr Alexander! The chaos that surrounded these gigs can be illustrated by a tale of what happened when the tour reached the ABC Blackpool just two nights later. The girls clamouring for the Walkers were using tactics that even hardened football fans would have baulked at. As mounted police tried to quell the storm outside, girls armed with handfuls of marbles rolled them under the hooves, causing the animals to buck, endangering both horse and rider. Meanwhile, a hysterical girl covered in blood being chased by a security guard near the stage was said to have crawled on her hands and knees through a broken window to get in.

Things were a little calmer at the De Montfort Hall, Leicester, the next night. The shows were a special moment for Engelbert in his home town. A total of forty-seven of his relatives were among an audience of 2,000 and the standing ovation that was given to his parents that night he described as the most emotional moment of his life.

Along with Cat Stevens and John Maus of the Walkers, Engelbert had also found a new hobby to while away the boredom of the dressing room hours – chess! Not very rock 'n' roll but Cat revealed that before their Lincoln show on 20 April there was money at stake – and that Humperdinck was looking likely to come out on top.

Cat was beginning to enjoy the limelight too. He told reporters that the tour was exceeding all expectations:

I feel my act is getting a lot better because I'm beginning to feel very much more at ease. My biggest shock came at Birmingham the other night [19 April] when I received a fan letter asking for my autograph, signed with 40,000 Pleases. It really hurt me. There were so many sheets of paper to the letter. I didn't think fans would go to that much trouble.

It was worth it, though. Cat duly dispatched his road manager to personally deliver the autograph.

By this time Cat and Engelbert had abandoned the tour bus ferrying them around the country. Cat was driving himself around in his Fiat and the stylish Humperdinck had taken to his Jag. There is always a price to be paid, however. Fans had started ripping off wing mirrors and windscreen wipers for souvenirs.

Between shows Cat, perhaps inspired by his song *I'm Gonna Get Me A Gun*, revealed he was writing a musical that ends in a gunfight. He enthused:

I haven't been commissioned to write it, but I'm hoping to sell it to some film company and then get offered the leading role. It's set in Mexico and tells the story of a guy from a rich family who runs away from home, falls in love with a girl and gets disillusioned when she steals a horse. In the end he has a gunfight with another guy.

Basically, it's about the good and bad in the world and the gunfight at the finish is meant to show whether he's become bad enough to draw first or not. I've written a few of the songs for it, including an Indian war dance sequence. That didn't require any musical research either. I just got the 'feel' for the number.

Cat was making a big impression on the tour too and offers were already coming in for him as the stars prepared to roll into Aldershot for their date at the ABC on Thursday 27 April.

... and so to Aldershot

Much to the annoyance of local reporter Steve Mann, security was watertight when the all-star show arrived at the ABC Cinema in Aldershot. So water tight, in fact, that Mann, the young irresistible force of the *Aldershot News*, was about to come up against an immovable object in the shape of tour publicist Brian Somerville.

Mann, who had brought along youngster Janice Parsonage, of Montgomery Road, Cove, to provide a 'teenager's viewpoint' for the newspaper, had made arrangements with Somerville to interview the stars, but Somerville proved implacable on the night.

The tone of Mann's subsequent report in the Young Ideas section of the newspaper reflected his resentment. Nothing was written of the performances, but plenty about the security. The headline 'Despite Objections, I Made It Backstage' summed up the mood. Mann complained:

In complete contrast to the Hollies/Small Faces show last autumn and last month's Orbison concert when our reporters were allowed full interviewing facilities, I found myself hampered by petty officialdom.

Despite having made previous arrangements I was subjected to a grilling from Mr Somerville. Janice was refused permission to see the Walkers at all.

It was not all bad news. After 25 minutes, Mann was finally allowed into the dressing room for a 10-minute chat with Walker John Maus. Mann picks up the story:

While I was chatting to John I also saw Scott Engel who wasn't in a fit state to talk to me! He spent the whole time slumped over a chair and having his neck massaged – the first house performance had exhausted him.

John Maus, in complete contrast to the Walkers' image of being difficult to talk to, was extremely helpful and said that although the group will not be doing any more tours – 'We're getting too old for them' – they have no intention of splitting up.

Maus had been impressed with security at the ABC but declared the bouncers to be 'a trifle rough', although pointing out that none of the girls who attempted to storm the stage during the Walkers' performance was hurt.

Despite the setbacks, there was a wonderful bonus for Mann and young Janice – a precious few minutes with the Jimi Hendrix Experience. Mann wrote:

The only people I really had a chance to speak to, apart from John Maus, were the Jimi Hendrix Experience. Jimi, Noel and Mitch were extremely pleased with their reception and said that the Aldershot crowd was one of the most enthusiastic of the whole tour. They signed about 30 autograph books and seemed really pleased to talk to me.

And there were some extra special moments for young Janice:

She really enjoyed the show and was especially pleased to meet the Jimi Hendrix Experience. She was delighted to find that bass-player Noel Redding was wearing a shirt in exactly the same material as her dress!

She also seems to have fallen in love with drummer Mitch and came away from the show the proud possessor of one of his drumsticks!

However, Mann's report finished pretty much as it started as he concluded:

I was unable to talk to Cat Stevens or Engelbert Humperdinck, although I made firm arrangements to interview both artists during the interval. This was, again, due to Mr Somerville, who flatly refused to let me see either of the stars.

The John Maus denial that the Walkers were breaking up was way off the mark. In fact, the group's split was formally announced shortly after the column appeared and Steve Mann referred to it the following week, pointing out that the news came just after the newspaper's deadline.

Mann's report didn't go down well with everyone. Two weeks later a letter was printed from three outraged teenagers, S. Lispin, L. Turpin and T. Shortall of Gloucester Road, Aldershot, under the heading 'Appalling Coverage'. Part of the letter read:

We were horrified by the appalling coverage given to the Walker Brothers show. Steve Mann complained that he was unable to talk to any of the artists. Then why didn't he give a commentary on the show instead of turning his article into an attack on the management?

Also, the one photograph shown was of a girl fan being carried bodily from the cinema. Not one photograph of either the Walker Brothers, Engelbert Humperdinck, the Jimi Hendrix Experience or Cat Stevens.

The show was a thoroughly good one, but the press coverage was quite appalling.

Mann was stung into giving this explanation:

The whole point of the article was to give a different view of the show. As most people who were interested in the artists would have attended, any comment of mine about the songs etc would have been superfluous.

Therefore, I tried to get information from the artists backstage, which would have been denied to most people at the show. Unfortunately, I was unable to do this because of the attitude taken by Mr Somerville.

His report may have disappointed fans at the time, but we are luckier today. Fans have stored away memories of what they witnessed on that momentous night and they have shared those memories with us.

As an added bonus, two star performers and one star reporter with the *NME* have also recalled their precious memories of that remarkable tour.

Keith Altham and that explosive opening night from Hendrix

London was a smaller place in the 1960s and a tiny, select band of enthusiastic young journalists found themselves in the very fortunate position of being right at the heart of the vibrant music scene.

A key member of that close-knit community was respected *NME* writer Keith Altham who had outgrown his early days as a raw recruit staffer at the million-selling teen magazine *Fabulous 208* to become a friend and confidant to some of the brightest stars on the planet.

Among these pals was Chas Chandler, and when the Animals bassist brought his new protégé over from the United States to launch him on an unsuspecting British public he couldn't wait to find out what Keith made of him.

Keith was so blown away by Jimi Hendrix that he initially feared that the American's awesome talent would go over the heads of the UK public. Keith went on to interview Jimi eight or nine times and was on hand to see some of his most amazing performances. Even better than that, however, Keith can be credited with playing a key part in one of Jimi's most spectacular stage stunts – the burning of the guitar. The occasion was the opening night of the Walker Brothers tour at the Finsbury Park Astoria in London and Keith retains a clear memory of what happened and why:

Jimi Hendrix lets rip at Aldershot on that eventful 1967 Walker Brothers Tour. (*Aldershot News*)

We were sitting around backstage in the dressing room – Jimi and the boys, Chas, road managers Gerry Stickells and Eric Barret, and me. So Chas says to me, you're a journalist, you work for the *NME*, how can we steal all the publicity? What can we do that will get all the headlines? And I said it's kind of difficult because the Who were already smashing up guitars on stage and the Move were smashing up TV sets. Jimi said under his breath 'maybe I could smash up an elephant' and I said it's a pity that you can't set fire to your guitar. I don't know why it even came into my head – probably because in the back of my mind I can recall Jerry Lee Lewis setting fire to his piano on stage in America to upstage Chuck Berry.

I said it, half thinking to myself it's not going to work, but there was a pause and then Chas sent Gerry out to get some lighter fuel. It didn't go up for the first one or two attempts, so Jimi went behind the amp to try to get it going, but it wouldn't go and there was a little pile of matches as I recall.

They put on some more lighter fuel and it took hold quite dangerously – quite effectively – and of course it caused absolute mayhem, not the least of which was the attitude of the Astoria's security officer. He went bananas when he saw Jimi waving a flaming guitar around his head and screamed at him that he'd never work on the circuit again. They were going to sue them – they were going to do this and they were going to do that.

As Jimi strolled off stage the stunned crowd watched in disbelief as tour staff rushed on to tackle the flaming guitar, and the accusations started.

Fortunately, Jimi and the team had an ally on the spot:

The agent at the time was Tito Burns who Jimi used to like because he knew that in Tito's long past he had an act with an accordian and a monkey, which Jimi thought was hilarious. And Tito got into the act because this security guy went up to him and said Hendrix would never appear there again. Tito had a word in Chas's ear and warned him. He said Look I've got to come in and pretend I'm really angry with Jimi. Tito didn't give a damn about what happened because he thought it was a great show. Chas said we've got to get this guitar out of here, because if they've got the guitar they've got the evidence. Anyway, Tito smuggled the guitar out under his raincoat. He appeared in Jimi's dressing room, did the wagging finger bit to a grinning Jimi and said That's it Jimi you're never going to work on the circuit again. You can't do that kind of thing – fire hazards – and you could just see the neck of Jimi's charred guitar poking out of the top of Tito's raincoat as he was making his exit out of the theatre.

Chas had got one of the roadies to bandage up Jimi's hands – although whether it was playing for the sympathy vote or a bit more drama for the newspapers I'm not too sure. He was supposed to be going to hospital to have his wounds dressed, that was the story. Of course they did nick all the press. It became a huge story.

Keith maintains that stories of Jimi regularly burning his guitar as part of the act are an exaggeration:

Everybody always expected him to set fire to his guitar thereafter, every time he played, but he didn't. He only did it three times in his life – once at the Astoria, once at the Saville Theatre and once at the Monterey Festival – all three of which I was actually present at. I remember Jimi saying to me at the Saville Theatre maybe you can set fire to your typewriter tonight, Keith. He was getting a bit fed up with it by then.

The tour represented the first glimpse of Hendrix in towns up and down the country – but the last of the Walkers, and Keith recalls the state Scott was in:

Scott, who I wrote quite a lot of stuff on, and I was his PR on two solo albums, was absolutely awestruck by Jimi. I remember going backstage one night and Scott saying to me What am I doing in the same company as someone like Jimi Hendrix? Scott was essentially a serious musician. He wanted to write. He wanted to do things that were avant-garde, which is what he does now, and has been doing for the last fifteen to twenty years. Seeing Jimi second or third on the bill to him just seemed to Scott like the most absurd thing he had ever come across. Here was this fantastic musician, while Scott was going on stage and singing *The Sun Ain't Gonna Shine Any More* and *My Ship Is Coming In* and he saw it as just being utterly ludicrous.

I don't think Jimi finished Scott, I think Scott just got to the stage where he was sick of the teenage idol problem. He'd had enough of being screamed at and regarded as a kind of sex symbol. It's quite fun for the first year, that kind of thing, but as every boy band has found out it wears off quite quickly and you either progress from that and get into something a little bit more adult, or you go under.

Scott was quite a reclusive character and he was terrified of live performance. When I was his PR I had to make up all kind of excuses for him sometimes to get him out of gigs because he was terrified of going out on stage. He was just one of those people who had stage fright.

Cat was holding his own on the tour, but Keith recalls him being a regular victim of the same Noel Redding prank. 'When Cat was singing *I'm Gonna Get me A Gun*, Noel used to squirt him from the wings with a water pistol. This jet of water would come shooting out of the curtains. Cat got quite annoyed about that after a while.'

Watch out, it's Walker mania!

It would not be an exaggeration to say that the giant void left in the mid-1960s teen scene when the Beatles decided to get serious with their music was filled by the Walker Brothers. In fact, it is hard to over estimate the impact the Walkers had on the hearts and minds of the nation's girls.

Drummer Gary Walker (Leeds) will never forget the craziness of those years:

Some nights we had to climb out of the window of the bus on to the roof because you couldn't get out of the doors and then the bus would drive away with us on the roof. Then you'd have girls that would sneak on the bus the night before and they'd be hiding everywhere. Then somebody would come into the dressing room and say I hate to bother you but there's a girl up in the lights who's gonna jump if you don't go out and see her. We'd go out there immediately – the police couldn't get them down.

In fact, the police would sometimes unwittingly hamper their exit as they bent a few rules of the road in their haste to get away. Gary recalled what happened to one inexperienced young copper:

Back then I wouldn't know if we played Birmingham or Manchester. They all eventually became the same place to us. The same aggro would happen and the police would stop your car when you were escaping. We drove up the hill this one time and cut in front of this bus. This policeman with a dog stopped us at the top of the hill. He said we'd cut the bus up and I tried to explain there's a bit of circumstances here. He just told me to be quiet and started to give us the lecture. I tried to talk but he shut me up and was threatening to give us a ticket or something and then I could see behind him about sixty girls running up the hill.

This was a younger policeman and he had no idea what was going to happen. So he's still talking away and the girls are getting closer and the dog's getting geed up and then you could see their faces – like the angry mob and the dog started to bark.

I tried to warn him and then I saw the girls come over him like a wave on a beach and he just disappeared and the dog and everything. I was more worried about the dog really, and that it might bite somebody.

Pop stars at the centre of such scenes always recall the lengths fans would go to – and in the Walkers' case even the disabled were not safe:

We would turn up early to set everything up and do the soundchecks. I said to this promoter one night What's that area there? He said it was

John Walker of the Walker Brothers in 1967. (Courtesy of the *Leicester Mercury*)

for the kids in wheelchairs. I said did he know there's quite a bit of excitement when we're playing. He wasn't worried. He said we've had the Beatles here and the Rolling Stones here but I was concerned and I went back and told Scott immediately. I said I don't think we ought to go on and he said go back and tell him.

I told the promoter we were concerned about the kids in the wheelchairs getting hurt and we might not go on if they don't sort it

Judging by the girls with hands over their ears, the Jimi Hendrix Experience are on stage ... or perhaps it's the screams for the **Walkers?** (*Aldershot News*)

The author with Gary Walker at the Sherlock Holmes pub in London, November 2006. (Author's collection)

The girls knew all the tricks. Whatever we tried, the girls were always one step ahead.

You never could escape and it got worse the further north you went. They seemed to get a little more desperate. I think it was Glasgow where we had to come in at 4 a.m. That was the only way they could guarantee that nobody would get hurt. We'd arrive at 4 a.m. and leave about 9 p.m. the next night.

The hysteria was incredible because they had this super strength. I remember one girl grabbed John's hair when we were going back from the performance to the hotel. It was Birmingham or Manchester – John got out of the car first and the girl grabbed his hair. She was about fifteen I suppose and small. But could they get her off him? It took about three bouncers. Eventually, John hit her in the face. Her eyes got real big and her mouth flew open and she just went oh and laughed. Anyway, I ran on and I ended up running this lady down in the lobby of the hotel. It was Marlene Dietrich. She'd never seen anything like that. John ran straight through the air because there were steps that he didn't go down and he hit his head. Everywhere you went it was the same. Getting in, getting out. The ambulance people would come out and tell all the girls in the first and second rows that if you do anything you're out. They always had quite a few ambulances because everybody was fainting. It was like a great big therapy thing – mass hysteria and screaming.

Drink could be a comfort when you were under siege:

The Walker Brothers liked drinking. If we went in at 4 a.m. we'd start drinking, then by the time 4 p.m. came we were speaking a foreign language. We didn't do drugs, just drink, but it didn't matter because nobody was going to hear anything anyway. Once you got out there you sobered up right away. Then when you came off stage it was a terrible thing.

Some pop stars coped better than others with the downside of that kind of fame. John thrived on the attention and Gary was not fazed by it, but number one heartthrob Scott was struggling to cope. 'It was fun being a Walker, but not for Scott,' said Gary. 'He preferred keeping private. What bothered Scott was being known. I think he was happy if people asked for an autograph and they liked your stuff – that's what he cared about, but the rest of it...'

It wasn't just fans Scott could be uncomfortable with:

On that 1967 tour, Jimi Hendrix would come into our dressing room, or we'd go to his, but not Scott. It'd be John and myself. And we'd sit around and just play and play. Jimi was a normal, regular guy, happy to mix in, but Scott would stay in there and he didn't want anybody in the dressing room.

It was just terrible nerves I think. Nobody can pin it down to anything else. If they say he was unfriendly well they're all wrong about that. He

out. With that he mentioned a lawsuit, so Scott says OK we've done everything we could.

When the show started I peeked out through the curtains and saw the wheelchairs there – about twelve of them – and they were fine. Then we came on and I just saw the crowd come forward and the wheelchairs disappeared. The curtain came down within about five seconds and the guy was running around backstage – his eyes as big as fried eggs – and he said he'd never seen anything like it. He said he'd had the Beatles there and this had never happened and I said I don't know what else to tell you. And you could just see the chairs tipped over and the wheels spinning. I'd tried to warn him. We got that hysteria.

When the Walkers first arrived in Britain they enjoyed the experience of the tour bus. 'We all wanted to be together and it was fun. The stories and the singing – you could do this and do that. I remember the Kinks on the first one and hearing about the two brothers fighting. I never got involved with that.' They soon graduated to cars as their fame grew, though. It made little difference. The girls targeted the cars now and the band resorted to tricks of their own – dressing up and decoy cars – but nothing worked. Gary said:

was just in such a shattered state. It must have just been stage fright. It was lucky I was there. I don't know what would have happened.

The Walkers broke up on that 1967 tour, but Gary does not blame Scott for the split:

We were all fine, that wasn't the problem. The management was the problem. We had two managers. One wanted to go one way and one wanted to go the other. I don't think they realised how big it was all going to get. I said well that's fine then, I'll do what I want to do.

The main management wanted Scott to be Frank Sinatra and Scott didn't wanna do it. And John was the lead singer originally – not Scott, and John wanted to do some of his things and of course I wanted to do a different thing entirely.

Gary recalls that Scott was not the only star to keep himself to himself. 'I saw less of Cat than people did Scott. You never saw him until he went on stage. Then he'd go on with the gun and that. I'd showed him how you can do all that stuff with the gun – draw quick and spin it and he liked all of that.'

Gary, who has been living all these years in England, was back in Walker Brother mode in 2006, promoting the re-released single *The Sun Ain't Gonna Shine Any More* and a Walkers' hits collection.

He also had projects in the pipeline:

(*Left*) **Now if you're going to point a gun at the audience you're going to get a reaction… The crowd just can't contain themselves as Cat Stevens is mobbed during** *I'm Gonna Get Me A Gun.* (*Aldershot News*)

(*Right*) **Security men move in to save a smothered Cat from his fans.** (*Aldershot News*)

I'm finishing writing some songs and then I want to co-write more songs with Joey Mollands of Badfinger and try to get a tour going as Gary Walker and the Rain 2.

I got a call from the Standells, the first group I was in before the Walkers. They have had their record Dirty Water put in the all time 500 most influential rock 'n' roll records and I will try to get something together with them also.

The excitement reaches fever pitch.
(*Aldershot News*)

Aldershot wasn't ready for what Jimi was wearing...

Teenage mod pals David Sands and Bryan Green were determined to grab the opportunity to see their hero Jimi Hendrix on that historic night in Aldershot.

Not so much of a problem for seventeen-year-old David, who was by then working at Gale and Polden, however, Bryan was still a Farnham Grammar schoolboy and as such had no chance of coming up with the shillings for that precious ticket. 'It was down to Plan B – I would have to bunk in,' Bryan confessed. 'The advice I'd been given was to go in with no jacket to make it look as if I was already in and had popped out – just walk in confidently.'

It worked and Bryan, then of North Lane, Aldershot, was able to join David, who lived nearby in Holly Road, for the show.

By that time Bryan had already had a tantalising glimpse of his hero. He recalled:

> I would travel home from school by bus, changing buses at a stop behind the cinema. I was on the top deck – it would have been about 4.30 p.m. – as the bus was pulling away from behind the cinema. As I looked down I saw a small crowd of people down near the old police station and I wondered what they were staring at.
>
> Then I saw Jimi, Mitch and Noel walking past Crail's the fruit and veg shop that was opposite the police station. Let me tell you, Aldershot was not ready for what they were wearing! They were outrageously psychedelic – all bright reds and florals – and what with Hendrix's hair, they were quite a sight. Hendrix was my hero and I was so frustrated that I couldn't jump off and get his autograph.
>
> Even though people were staring, nobody pestered them. They were just able to walk up the road on their own.

Though ticket-less, Bryan waited at home for David to call round on his scooter – a white Vespa SS180 – for that all-important ride back into town for the big gig. First stop was their regular mod meeting place – Macari's – in those days in Victoria Road where Buy-Lo is now. 'Macari's closed at 9 p.m. but we would hang around for about an hour afterwards on our scooters,' said Bryan. There was to be no hanging about on this occasion; they quickly moved on to the Pegasus pub opposite the ABC. The cinema was

already busy, with queues building outside. 'We got to the pub about 8 p.m. I suppose,' said Bryan. 'We managed to get served though we weren't really old enough.'

As the boys walked in they saw a famous name who was not on the bill, looking rather the worse for wear:

> We found what appeared to be a very drunk Peter Noone sitting at a table in the corner talking to a girl. We must have been told he was in there I suppose. Then it was a case of find something for him to sign.
>
> All I had was a Number Six cigarette coupon so I went over and presented him with that and he signed Cheers, Herman. I remember getting an autograph for someone else too who was too shy to go up, even though he fancied himself as a bit of a hard man.
>
> I remember Herman having to be helped out of the pub by people with him. He could only have been about eighteen or nineteen.

A friend of David and Bryan's, Sue Masters, who lived near them in Friend Avenue and worked at Barclays Bank in Aldershot at the time, was also in the pub. She was about to go to the concert with a friend. Sue recalled, 'Peter Noone certainly appeared to be pretty drunk. I remember he kept saying to this girl "So your name's Pitt", repeating it over and over.'

Somehow David, Bryan and Sue all got in for the show. Bryan recalled:

> The first people I saw were the Californians. I hadn't heard of them before, but they were quite good – sort of Beach Boys style. I remember a little fair-haired guy singing.

Sue also remembers 'the little fair haired guy' as she plucked up the courage to chat him up after the show:

> I thought he was lovely. As they were packing up I jumped on to the bus and got talking. It must have

David Sands in the 1960s. (Courtesy of David Sands)

Bryan Green in 1967. (Courtesy of Bryan Green)

Sue Masters in the 1960s. (Courtesy of Sue Masters)

gone pretty well because he said he would put a ticket on the door for me the next night – at Slough I think it was – and I was dead chuffed.

But of course I couldn't get there in the end. Slough? It might as well have been New York! I remember phoning the venue the next night and saying can you leave a message for him that Sue from Aldershot can't be there and she's really sorry. As if he would have cared. I doubt that he would even have remembered.

Bryan Green, Sue Masters and David Sands in 2006. (Author's collection)

The show, of course, was memorable. Bryan said:

I remember Cat Stevens in his dark green jacket. He put on a holster – which I thought was quite corny – to sing *I'm Gonna Get Me A Gun*. But he was quite good though. He had to be good live to reproduce the sound of his records, but I was mainly there to see the Jimi Hendrix Experience. They played *Purple Haze* and *Hey Joe*. In the middle of *Hey Joe* he started playing the guitar with his teeth and then during another number – I can't remember which – he started playing *Strangers In The Night*. It sounded like a violin. It still sticks with me to this day. It was awesome.

Less memorable for David, Bryan and Sue were the Walker Brothers and Humperdinck – who were not their cup of tea – but, of course, they recall the screaming.

The fun did not end with the show. Bryan, David and Sue hung around afterwards under a side window to the dressing room. Bryan remembered:

Jimi put his head out every now and again. We just waited and waited. One of the Experience chucked us down a drink so we were pretty chuffed. By this time most people had gone home, apart from the die-hard idiots like us.

After about half an hour or so they started emerging out of the back to load the gear into the coach. That's when I saw Sue in there talking to one of the Californians. A drunken squaddie came

up to Jimi Hendrix and was going on about how great he thought Jimi was – I don't expect he had even been to the show. He was probably on his way from the pub! Anyway, Jimi was very polite. Then we managed to talk to Jimi, and David and I both got his autograph. What a trophy that was to take to school the next day!

Then we jumped on our scooters – me and David on his and Sue on the back of a friend's – and followed the bus out of town. It went up Hospital Hill and on towards the Farnborough Road. I think we followed it about as far as the Queens Hotel – sometimes drawing up alongside. Jimi and the boys were in the back and they waved at us several times. We were starstruck I suppose, but it was great fun.

David recalls:

Jimi was really friendly. He was obviously used to people coming up to him and he was very willing to sign autographs for people – in fact, he seemed pleased to.

Bryan, David and Sue are all still living locally.

Another in the crowd under the dressing room window that night was David Paul, who had turned up for a glimpse of the stars of the Roy Orbison show three weeks before. He also recalls Hendrix in a friendly mood chatting to the fans gathered under the window.

David, then sixteen and living in the family home in Angelsey Road, Aldershot, was also a proud member of the local mods. With his own scooter, he was another regular at that popular meeting place, Macari's, and he too did not have enough shillings to get into the show.

Colin Phillips celebrated his fourteenth birthday that night by getting the No.12 bus from the family home in Hartley Wintney to Aldershot with his mates to join the throng at the side of the cinema:

I can't think that my dad would have been very pleased if he'd known, but I probably just told him I was going to the pictures. It was the sort of excuse I'd come up with.

There were quite a few people who couldn't get tickets and they had just gone along to listen outside. We thought we might as well join them – we'd hang around listening and hope to get to see Hendrix. People were quite excited to see him in Aldershot.

Their perseverance paid off:

Jimi did come out at some point. I'm sure he was wearing a hat. He went across the road and either went to the pub [Pegasus] or the chip shop – but I'm sure he came out. We didn't realise at first, but then somebody spotted him.

Colin went to several of the ABC concerts – but this was the only time he did not have a ticket:

I was definitely at the Hollies show and I remember enjoying it, although I would have been disappointed that the Small Faces didn't appear. One of my mates told me about a week before that he had a spare ticket and did I want to go? The Hollies and Manfred Mann were among my favourites.

I was quite impressed with Paul Jones – possibly because it was a solo performance without Manfred Mann.

David Paul and his scooter. (Courtesy of David Paul)

Jimi's first note almost took the roof off the old Odeon

The fact that Phil Marsden and his mate Michael Hubbard were only seventeen was not going to stop them popping over the road to the pub to celebrate after they watched the first house of the Walker Brothers package at the Leeds Odeon.

The cheeky pair persuaded the barman to pour their pints and then looked over in amazement to see Jimi Hendrix and Mitch Mitchell surrounded by admirers at the next table. Phil, who was at Ossett Grammar School, retaking his O-Levels, said:

> I've never forgotten it. There was an entourage with Jimi and Mitch, but Jimi was sat there happily signing autographs for the girls. We recognised him immediately because we'd just seen him on stage!

Phil Marsden in November 2006. (Courtesy of Phil Marsden)

After a while one of the entourage said 'Okay girls, that's enough' and the girls got up and went and that's when I got the first clear look at Jimi. He looked a bit odd to us, with his big fluffy hair and everything. People weren't used to seeing that then.

Michael said that he thought Jimi looked a bit like a bus conductor because of what he was wearing – somehow I couldn't imagine Jimi on the buses!

After a few minutes the pub door went again and more girls came in. They came up to him and must have asked for autographs because he asked if anyone had a pen. I had one in my pocket and so I gave that to him and when he finished signing for them he signed an autograph for me.

When he finished signing, he started chain-smoking.

As for his performance that night, it was amazing. I'd never heard anything like it. His first number was *Purple Haze* and the first note about took the ceiling off. The power and volume of that performance was like nothing I'd heard before. I was just in awe of him.

Hey Joe was just going out of the charts, I think, but he played that as well, and *Wind Cries Mary* and *Foxy Lady*. I'd gone there to see the Walker Brothers, but I came away thinking about Hendrix. I bought their album *Are You Experienced* the very next day, but I don't know what happened to the autograph.

Phil was also impressed with Cat Stevens:

> He was wearing the cowboy stuff for *I'm Gonna Get Me A Gun* and that was good. He'd had two or three songs in the charts by then so we knew him.

Phil has long since moved from the village of Ossett, about ten miles from Leeds, where he was living then. He now lives in Leicester, so what were his memories of Engelbert Humperdinck?

> Well I know a lot more about him now that I've been living in Leicester all these years. His music wasn't to my taste, and it still isn't really, but I do remember this little old lady sat next to me standing

(*Left*) **Michael Hubbard 1967.** (Courtesy of Phil Marsden and Michael Hubbard)

(*Right*) **Phil Marsden in 1967.** (Courtesy of Phil Marsden)

up when he sang *Release Me* and the tears were just streaming down her face, so the song obviously meant something to her.

Engelbert must have been closing the first half because I remember that she didn't come back in after the interval.

A stroll in the park with Jimi Hendrix

Sunday was a good day for your town to host the big pop show – there was no school and it meant you could get along nice and early to catch the stars arriving.

Jennifer Toseland and her pals did exactly that when the Walker Brothers package was due at the De Montfort Hall in Leicester on Sunday 16 April 1967. The big idea, of course, was to meet their Walker idols, but the early birds ended up chatting with Jimi Hendrix and his mates instead:

We would have got there around 4 p.m. Jimi was outside in the gardens chatting and signing autographs. With his long sheepskin coat and big hair, he appeared enormous. We spoke to him. We weren't too impressed to be meeting him, of course, but he was very friendly and polite. He was with his band and all three signed a piece of paper for me.

I know we booked the tickets as soon as they went on sale because we got the third row, and the first two rows were mainly for Engelbert's family! It was great. It meant we were near enough to get to the stage. Engelbert's relatives were of all ages and they were pretty disgusted when we all got up and screamed and tried to climb over them when the Walkers came on. They shushed us and tried to get us to sit down and stop screaming, but that was not going to happen.

It was absolutely brilliant. Of course, we couldn't hear much of the music because of all the screaming, but there were two speakers on either side of the stage and every time the Walker Brothers jumped up on them everybody went wild.

Cat Stevens was a bit of a newcomer for us, but I enjoyed his songs that night.

Jennifer was a fourteen-year-old pupil of Alderman Newton Girls' Grammar School and lived on the New Parks estate in Leicester. She is now Jennifer Bown and still lives in Leicestershire, in the village of Huncote.

I was pretty young to have been there, I suppose, but my eldest sister had been to see the Beatles in Leicester a few years before when I was too young to go, so I suppose I must have nagged my parents.

We would probably have been dropped off and then picked up at the end, but it was all very exciting.

I found the ticket and autographs several years ago, and my children were more impressed than I was. My daughter now has them framed in her home and they are considered a family heirloom!

Jennifer Toseland in the 1960s before she became Jennifer Bown. (Courtesy of Jennifer Bown)

Jennifer Bown (*née* Toseland) in 2006. (Courtesy of Jennifer Bown)

Lorraine's close encounter with a guitar hero

Schoolgirl Lorraine Bray had an advantage over the other girls trying to get backstage to meet the Walker Brothers at the De Montfort Hall, Leicester – she knew the venue inside out.

Lorraine, then fourteen, had sung many times in a school choir and rehearsed for concerts there. So, with perfect timing, as the Walkers were about to launch into their final number, Lorraine made a beeline for the Green Room and out into the foyer at the back before the security men were in place, but instead of meeting her idol Scott, she ended up in a close encounter with a guitar legend:

While the Walkers were still playing I ran as fast as I could to the back of the hall and made my way through to the back of the stage. I left my friend behind and said I'd meet her later because she wouldn't have been able to keep up – it was every girl for herself!

There were no security guys there and as I waited it was Jimi Hendrix who came down the stairs. I

Lorraine Worley in 2006. (Courtesy of Lorraine Worley)

remember being a bit frightened of him. He was quite a big man, tall, and he was wearing a flame orange shirt with frilly ruffles down the front, and stripey trousers. He was sweaty and had a bottle of beer in his hand.

He was with a group of women. One was blonde and wearing a short, cowskin coat and miniskirt. They were groupies, I suppose. But Jimi was very nice to me.

He asked where I was going, and I said I was waiting to see Scott. He said 'You don't wanna see him – he's a depressive. Will I do?'

Then he said 'By the way, did you like my music?' I said yeah, it was OK, but I still wanted to see Scott. Then this bouncer said I would have to leave and Jimi said 'Hey man, leave her alone – she's my sister'.

The women didn't say anything when he was talking to me, but he was just interested in his music and what I thought of it. He gave me a kiss and an autograph.

Although I felt intimidated when I first saw him he quickly made me feel comfortable. He was warm and genuine.

Lorraine may still have been clutching the knitted hearts she had made for Scott, but at least Jimi would have appreciated her purple coat – and she looked suitably lairy too in her white lipstick and black eye make-up. 'I shouldn't have been there really – I was only fourteen. I was too young for everything, but still wanted to do it all.'

Once Jimi left, the bouncer finally persuaded Lorraine to leave and she was soon aware of the baying teenagers outside.

Lorraine's family home is in Ayelestone, Leicester, but she now lives in Bristol. Now Lorraine Worley, she is a musician and classical singing teacher, but recalls the desperate measures she took to secure her ticket to the big concert all those years ago when she was still a pupil at St Jonathan's Girls School:

My father hadn't been well and the family was struggling financially. Then a friend came up with the idea of breeding rabbits – you could sell them to the butchers. People did things like that back then.

Lorraine Worley, then Lorraine Bray, in the 1960s aged fourteen. (Courtesy of Lorraine Worley)

I managed to breed two rabbits. I gave one away, but I was desperate to see the Walkers and there was no way the family had enough money to get me a ticket.

So in the end I took the other one down to the butchers and sold him. I got about 10s 6d – just about what I needed for the ticket. The funny thing is the rabbit's name was Lucky Star!

I was so lucky to win my ticket for the big show

The big treat for Maureen Hayler was to meet up with her friends and go to Farnborough Town Hall for the pop shows. Among the stars she saw were the Who, Manfred Mann, Millie and Dave Dee, Dozy, Beaky, Mick and Tich, but on another big night, at the ABC Cinema in Aldershot, eighteen-year-old Maureen took her seat for the Walker Brothers.

It tasted all the sweeter too because Maureen's ticket was free, a nice bonus for a teenage girl short of money:

> I won a competition. I can't remember what it was, but I was so chuffed when the ticket arrived. I felt privileged to be there for a show like that and I didn't even have to pay!

Maureen Saywood and her daughter Beth in 2006.

Others were there to see their particular favourite, but Maureen was excited at the prospect of seeing them all:

> It was just magical. To see all those stars in the flesh playing just for us was amazing.
>
> My favourite was Cat Stevens. I liked the way he sang – the feeling he put into it, and the songs were meaningful. He sat there playing his guitar. I liked his songs and the way he performed them.
>
> But then I liked the Walkers for other reasons – especially the blond one [Scott]. It's funny how at that age looks are everything and it's only later on that you realise they are not the most important thing. Girls always go for the good looking ones, even though they are often the ones who hurt you most!

Engelbert was a favourite with the mums, but eighteen-year-old Maureen was quite taken too:

> I liked him. I liked his long sideburns. He was a handsome man. The stars were all so different, but I genuinely liked them all. I'm sure I would have gone even if I hadn't won the ticket.

It was Jimi Hendrix who left the most lasting impression:

> His music was so different. No one else will ever play the guitar like that. Jimi Hendrix was a wild man. He played the guitar with his teeth and behind his back – he was fantastic. It wouldn't surprise me if he had been high on drugs because of what we now know about him, but he was brilliant.

Because Maureen won her ticket she went to the concert alone, rather than with her usual friends:

Maureen Saywood, then Maureen Hayler, in the 1960s.
(Courtesy of Maureen Saywood)

> I was sitting upstairs in the balcony looking down on the left of the stage. It was a great view. I would have gone to the later show because I went there on the bus and came back in a taxi. It was safer for a girl on her own at that time of night, even in those days.
>
> But everything about that night was magical – the atmosphere especially. I'm sure I was screaming with all the rest. It was the best concert I ever went to.

These days Maureen Saywood and a mother of five girls, she still lives in Farnborough, just a few streets from where she grew up in Lye Copse.

Annette – the girl with the signed programme!

Annette Syms was nineteen-year-old Annette Dean living at the family home in Cargate Avenue, Aldershot, when the Walker Brothers tour rolled into town.

Annette was not fazed about being around musicians – she was going out with the singer of local group the Condors – and her friend Ann, who accompanied her to the ABC Cinema that night, was already married to the group's drummer. That aside, the girls were in a state of excitement when they met up after work and contemplated seeing their idols – the Walker Brothers – in the flesh. Annette recalled:

> We both liked the Walkers, especially Scott. We just idolised him. Their music was great too and I also liked Engelbert and Cat, but I didn't care for Jimi Hendrix. To be honest, at the time I couldn't wait for him to get off so we could see the Walker Brothers.

Nevertheless, all these years later, it is of Jimi Hendrix that Annette talks most proudly to her children. She has a wonderful memento: the original programme signed by the Walkers, Humperdinck and Hendrix. The front page contains pictures of the three Walkers with their signatures, in biro, on each. The programme is now stored safely away in a bank vault!

> I can't remember exactly when the programme was signed, but my best guess is that it was at the end of the show. I think I took it down into the foyer and someone from security or a staff member took it back into the dressing room where they all were.
>
> I was so excited about the Walkers signing the cover that I didn't bother opening it up. It was some time before I realised that Jimi and Engelbert had signed too!

Annette was an Army typist at the Officer Cadet School in Mons Barracks, Aldershot, so it would have been a quick pop home to get cleaned up and changed before strolling down to Ann's house in Victoria Road on the way to the cinema. Annette recalls the excitement:

> There was such an atmosphere. Everybody was on a high. To have the Walker Brothers there we thought was quite something. Everybody was making a racket

Annette Syms in the 1960s. (Courtesy of Annette Syms)

Annette Syms in the 1960s. (Courtesy of Annette Syms)

– clapping, cheering and screaming. Everything was so loud – it had to be to hear the singing and music over all that.

Did Annette join in?

Oh yes. I had been to concerts before where I was screaming like mad, but that was at school. Ann was three or four years older and a bit more mature, but when the Walkers came on everybody was screaming and when I saw Ann screaming I just joined in!

Before the Walkers came on in the second half there was a scare:

Our seats were upstairs. I remember something being said, probably from the stage, that there might be some sort of problem with the Walkers – maybe we got talking to other people in the audience. Anyway, there was some sort of doubt that they would appear.

The girls could only watch and wait in the first half as they settled back in their seats:

Cat Stevens came on. I quite liked him and would sing along to his records, but I don't recall much of his performance. It was the same with Engelbert, but people were singing along and I remember enjoying it.

Then it was time for Jimi Hendrix:

He was so loud. I vaguely remember people around us putting hands over their ears. When he played *Purple Haze* the whole place seemed to go purple – I don't know if it was lighting or a steam machine, but everything went purple when he played that song.

He played the guitar behind the back of his neck and with his teeth, but I wasn't impressed. I just couldn't wait for the Walkers!

Cue pandemonium when they emerged:

Despite the screaming, we sang along because they were mainly ballads and we knew all the words.

All the girls had pushed down the front and were stretching out and trying to touch them, but I don't recall the Walkers going down into the crowd and touching people like Robbie Williams does today.

Upstairs, we had a good view. We could see the whole stage. I came out absolutely exhausted and we had no voices left, but it was brilliant. I can still remember it all these years on and I've been to hundreds of shows since then.

Annette Syms in 2006. (Author's collection)

I was there for the Walkers, but at least I can look back and say I saw Jimi Hendrix in Aldershot. Even my children couldn't believe it.

That was the only Aldershot ABC show Annette attended, but she did pick up the autographs of the Rockin' Berries at the stage door when they played there that November.

Annette has never fallen out of love with music and shamelessly states that she has played the Ministry of Sound so loud her daughter has asked her to turn it down!

Grand finale when the drums went flying

Debbie Lockwood was a young mum of twenty-three years old who had only ever been to one concert before she saw the all-star Jimi Hendrix/Walker Brothers show.

Like so many of the females at the ABC Aldershot that night, Debbie was more excited at the prospect of seeing the Walkers and Humperdinck than this little-known American rock star with the giant frizzy hair, outrageous clothes and a penchant for playing the guitar with his teeth:

> I was working at the old Ministry of Social Security in Aldershot – it's known as the benefits agency now. There was a young colleague – Penny I think her name was – who got the tickets. She had ginger hair and wore thick black rimmed glasses, as many of the girls did then, but she was a real live wire.
>
> Six or eight of us went along. We would all have been about the same age and we didn't need much persuading.

Even better, live wire Penny pulled off a real coup – front row seats. 'They were slightly to the right as you looked at the stage. It was a great view.'

Debbie Lockwood pictured by the author.

The girls' office in Pickford Street was a short walk from the cinema. They finished work at 5.30 p.m. and headed down for the first house at 6.15 p.m.

Although Engelbert and the Walkers were Debbie's favourites, it was Jimi Hendrix who made the big impression:

> There was this guy with the big hair and lairy clothes lying on his back playing the guitar – playing with his teeth and then with the guitar behind him. It was amazing.
>
> We didn't know much about Jimi Hendrix, so it was quite a surprise. It was quite spectacular. He was in a class of his own.
>
> I probably watched it open mouthed – enjoying it, but feeling a little bit shocked at the same time.

Debbie, who still lives in Aldershot, was shocked by the finale:

> The drummer smashed his drums. He was in a frenzy, hitting them so hard. They just fell apart and were left like it I think. The curtain came down. It was the end, but I'm not sure it was deliberate.

However impressed Debbie and her friends were with the antics of the Experience, it was the heart throbs they had really come to see:

> Engelbert was gorgeous. I could have gone for him. He was sexy for those days. He was teasing us, of course, taking off his waistcoat and swinging it over his head. He knew he had what it took. We would all have been up screaming for him. But we would only have screamed for him and the Walkers.

Debbie was fond of Cat Stevens' songs and the girls gave him a good reception as they waited for their favourites.

There was a shock in store for Debbie and most of the audience, though, when it was announced from the stage that the Walkers were to stop touring:

> We were all devastated. We loved them and their music and for us to watch them here – nothing like this ever happened in Aldershot – and then

Debbie Lockwood in the 1960s with her daughter Micki.
(Courtesy of Debbie Lockwood)

to hear at the same time that they were breaking up was such a disappointment. But they were very smart and very professional. We were probably screaming through all their nice harmonies, which is a shame, but with the sad news, it left us with a real bittersweet taste.

That was the second and last concert that Debbie has been to. The first – at Wembley – featured Dusty Springfield, Cliff Richard and Billy Fury a few years before when she was sixteen. All in all she saw quite a few household names on just two big nights.

A heavily outnumbered guard looks like he wished he had a walkie-talkie to call for back-up. (*Aldershot News*)

Great Scott, it's scream queen Pauline

Eighteen-year-old Pauline Hall was not impressed when her mum told her they were leaving Surbiton at the back end of 1966 to begin a new life in Farnborough.

Mum had tired of the long coach journeys to Hampshire to work at Solartron and so the decision was made; however, for Pauline (now Pauline White), this was not good news. She recalled:

Surbiton was all I'd ever known. All my friends were there, and all the haunts where I used to hang out were there. All the nightlife was there – not that I had much money to spend.

I didn't know what to expect in Farnborough. I didn't think there would be much there, and of course I would miss my friends.

Pauline knuckled down and joined her mum at Solartron, and there was a bonus when they secured tickets for the pop show at the ABC Cinema in Aldershot.

Mum was looking forward to seeing Engelbert, but Pauline only had eyes for the Walkers (surprise, surprise, especially Scott!):

Pauline White, pictured by the author in 2006.

I loved the Hollies and the Beatles, but the Walker Brothers were right up there too and I was very excited.

I was very shy in those days, but I used to get hyped up before a show. Mum warned me not to start screaming because she would be embarrassed if I became hysterical.

I tried to contain myself, but once the Walkers came out, that was it! The noise of the screaming was just deafening. I don't think you could hear them over it. I remember standing on the seats and screaming. I was trying to behave myself for mum, but with the atmosphere... I just went along with it.

Pauline recalls that Cat Stevens attracted his share of screams:

He sort of exploded on to the stage. I remember the gun and holster. He went down very well. I quite liked his music.

Pauline was something of a pop music expert, having worked for a record shop in Kingston:

I knew all the bands, and the songs. I used to listen to Radio Luxembourg and then Radio Caroline, so when someone came into the shop and couldn't think of the title they wanted, I invariably knew it when they started singing or humming it. I missed all that, and the concert in Aldershot was the first good thing that happened.

I bought some new black, patent shoes for the show, and I was very proud of them. Mum was looking forward to going too. I wasn't a big fan of Engelbert, but mum loved him. Engelbert got a good reception and I know that mum enjoyed it. You could see it in her face when he came on. The rest of the show was so loud, but she put up with that.

Loudest of all was Hendrix, of course. Definitely one for daughter, rather than mum:

Like everyone else, I remember him playing the guitar with his teeth. I thought it was great. I

Pauline White, or Pauline Hall as she was in the 1960s. (Courtesy of Pauline White)

knew all about Jimi from my record shop days and I'd heard him on the radio. He was good that night.

Farnborough must have grown on Pauline a bit – she's still living there!

Hip Cat was gunning for the audience

Teenager Jenny Latimer of Carfax Avenue, Tongham, and her boyfriend (now husband) Tony Boxall were there at the Aldershot cinema to witness Cat Stevens and his six shooter, but it was Jimi Hendrix who had one little girl diving for cover.

Cat went for his gun to add dramatic effect as he sang *I'm Gonna Get Me A Gun*, which was at six in the charts. Tony said:

> We came to enjoy the whole thing really, but Cat and Jimi were the two we were most looking forward to. Cat was wearing a bottle green suit with a waistcoat and I went out and bought an identical one shortly afterwards!

Cat's natty suit is captured in several pictures in this book as he whipped up a frenzy on stage. However, in one photograph he has discarded the jacket and is crouching to take aim with the pistol at an excited audience. The holster is clearly visible at his hip.

Tony and Jenny, who were downstairs about halfway back, recalled that Hendrix got a decent reception in the home of the Army – well, apart from one group of young men. Tony takes up the story:

> There were about half a dozen Sandhurst cadets in the row in front of us – Hooray Henry types. They weren't in uniform but the cadets always dressed

in a certain way – blazer and trousers – even when they were in civvies. And they were barracking Jimi. They considered the Experience to be oiks I suppose, but they were drowned out.

> When Jimi got going playing the guitar with his teeth or behind his neck the place went absolutely ballistic – except the Hooray Henrys who just sat there.

Jenny added:

> One lady near us was with her daughter. They must have been there to see Engelbert because the little girl dived under her seat when Jimi started playing. She was terrified.

Jenny and Tony also have memories of the bill toppers. Jenny said, 'It was great to see the Walker Brothers. They were *it* at that time. I liked them – especially Scott.'

Tony chimes in, 'They didn't do a lot for me!'

The overall memory, as ever, was of the hysteria. Jenny recalled:

> Everyone was screaming when Jimi was on, but also for the Walkers of course. But I don't remember so much screaming when Cat was on – you could hear the songs.

If that show provides an enduring fond memory, there was an incident that brings back far less pleasant memories for Jenny:

> I had a ticket to see the Beatles when they were appearing in Guildford in 1963. But then I got grounded for a month. My dad said That's it, you're not going to that concert, and I said, Oh yes I am. I hid the ticket, but they found it and I never did get to see the Beatles. My friends went, but I missed out. I've never forgotten that and I don't think I ever will.

Tony and Jenny Boxall pictured at their Aldershot home by the author in November 2006.

Tony and Jenny in the 1960s. (Courtesy of Tony and Jenny Boxall)

The tux, the bow-tie ... there's only one Engelbert. (*Aldershot News*)

Eight
Engelbert On Tour

Please release him!

THE POP WORLD underwent some monumental changes in 1967. *Sergeant Pepper's Lonely Hearts Club Band*, the album released by the Beatles on Thursday 1 June, set the scene for the summer of love and at a stroke took the art of recording music to yet another level. The marker had been set. From now on the top bands wanted to spend more time in the studio, crafting and perfecting their songs, as the novelty of running the gauntlet of screaming, half-crazed girls in gut-busting UK tours was rapidly wearing off.

The days of the packaged pop tour were numbered. In that autumn of 1967 many groups had had enough of spending endless hours on coaches and even more hanging around theatres waiting, bored, for their 20 minutes in the spotlight.

The Hollies were the latest group to announce they were quitting package tours – and falling attendances across the country suggested that fans were tiring of the format too.

The opening night of the Traffic/Vanilla Fudge tour was an unmitigated disaster, with all manner of things going wrong – from faulty equipment and bored bands to curtains dropping halfway through a performance. It was all too much for Traffic's drummer, Jim Capaldi, who said:

There have been too many tours. Audiences have seen too many artists run on for 20 minutes and go off again, with a rotten compère coming on at intervals.

No wonder they're cold and fed up. I'd like to see the style of tours that are going round now abolished. After that opening night, we nearly walked out. We thought Vanilla Fudge had a rough time. The whole thing was terrible. Then we had Chesterfield, which was just as bad.

Capaldi made the point that 20 minutes was hardly enough for musicians to showcase their talent and he called for tours limited to two acts, playing a half each. However, singers like Tom Jones and Engelbert Humperdinck were bucking the trend. Music fashions may have changed, but the summer of love and student demonstrations against the Vietnam War were lost on the mums and daughters (and occasional dads) who filled many of the seats at their shows.

Engelbert's fans were still more than happy to shell out their money for a chance to watch him in the flesh. The Humperdinck package tour that set out on a mammoth thirty-four-date slog up and down the country from late October 1967 did not even pretend to be about cutting-edge music. This was cabaret, pure and simple; and as if to labour the point, when Engelbert's voice went and he had to miss a couple of shows, cosy comedians Terry Scott and Hugh Lloyd were drafted in to replace him at the Winter Gardens in Bournemouth!

The line-up for the tour indicates that it really was the Engelbert show. The Rockin' Berries were the one concession to rock 'n' roll (and even they had more than a sprinkling of comedy in their act), with the Trebletones and the Staggerlees on the undercard. Anita Harris appeared on the opening night up until 11 November at the Gaumont in Taunton. The American Shirley Bassey-style singer Gigi Galon took over for the second half of the tour, which ended at the Liverpool Empire on Sunday 3 December. Television personality Lance Percival was also part of the package, and Johnny Temple was the compère.

A handbill from Engelbert's late 1967 tour still in the possession of the former cinema staff.

I'm not trying to be flash, but with the car I shall be able to rest when I want to, lie-in in the mornings if I feel like it, and feel a lot more relaxed.

The parts I am dreading are the long hauls, from Dublin to Aldershot for instance, where we may well have to travel right through the night.

Again, with short jumps to a town only a stone's throw away there is the whole day to do nothing – and there is nothing to do. I enjoy looking at the different towns we go through, and the different accents are marvellous, but I guess I shall spend every morning in bed.

Humperdinck, ever the professional, would arrive at a theatre long before the show so he could check out the acoustics, lighting and even the colour of the backcloth. Before the tour he had a week of rehearsals with his backing group – who he dubbed the Band of Men – supported by a brass section.

The star was still a dab hand at chess, but this time he arranged for a portable television for the tour so he could watch his own television show in the dressing room.

The thirty-four dates meant sixty-eight concerts and Engelbert knew he would have to prepare well to be at his best. While plenty of rock stars were experimenting with mind-bending hard drugs, his luggage contained nothing more sinister than his own remedy for warding off the dreaded winter cold: 'I shall take my Haliborange tablet every day. It really works, you know,' he told one reporter. 'On tour you're forever working and getting hot, then sitting down getting cold, and it's very easy for your resistance to break down.'

The tour began on Thursday 26 October, at the Adelphi in Slough. It was to set a pattern that was repeated throughout the tour, for the next five weeks: tearful mums and screaming daughters, with Engelbert the object of their emotions. Peeping through the curtains from the wings on that opening night, a nervous Anita Harris noted that there did not seem to be a single man in the audience. So daunted was she that she dropped her current hit *Playground* for fear of messing it up.

This really was a variety show. Lance Percival was a television entertainer (throwing in an impression of Bruce Forsyth along with the gags) and the Rockin' Berries broke up their music with knockabout custard pie routines, jokes and mimics thrown in.

Humperdinck had the limelight to himself, however. In a tuxedo on that opening night, he hit straight into *Shake* as the curtains parted, then relaxed into his ballads, selecting numbers like *There Goes My Everything*, *Ten Guitars*, *Yours Until Tomorrow* and *If It Comes To That*. He even picked up a boater for his own impression – of Frankie Vaughan.

Then as the Band Of Men played the 'Stripper' he wound the women into a frenzy by removing his bow-tie and jacket to reveal a snazzy red-backed waistcoat, and launched into *Place In The Sun* and *I Know* before landing the coup de grâce – *Release Me*.

Engelbert, with *The Last Waltz* already dancing towards a million sales, was by now a veteran of the exhausting pop tour and he was forsaking the claustrophobia of the tour bus for the freedom of the open road in his Jag, with road manager Tony Cartwright as chauffeur. He protested:

The Rockin' Berries – minus custard pies – in their Aldershot dressing room. (*Aldershot News*)

Introducing, fresh from the Talk of the Town, America's Shirley Bassey... Gigi Galon. (*Aldershot News*)

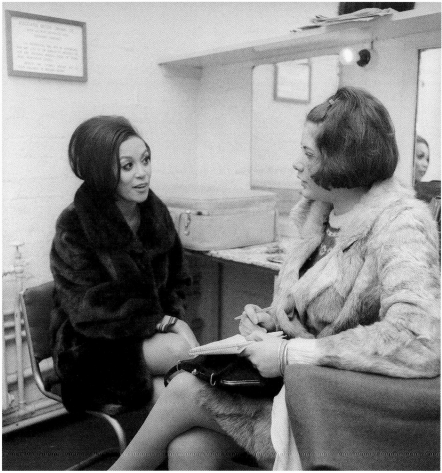

However, even with Engelbert's careful preparation, there was always bound to be the odd hiccup, and it was not long in coming. In fact, it came the very next night as the tour party arrived in Northampton to play the town's ABC Cinema.

Pop stars got used to dodging a flying fist (or even the odd flying glass) on these tours where the public got much closer to them than today, but waiting for Engelbert in his dressing room that night was a piece of hate mail so threatening that it led to security being beefed up for the rest of the tour. The unsigned letter, addressed to Dear Pretty Face, went on: 'My girl has left me as a result of you. We will see what your pretty face looks like after a bottle of acid. Watch out for the acid, or a knife in your back.'

Engelbert was toughing it out in the music papers that week, replying: 'I reckon I can look after myself, and if anyone comes menacingly within five yards of me during the next few weeks, he will be biting off more than he can chew.'

Manager Gordon Mills, however, was taking no chances. Police were swarming all over the Northampton cinema that night, watching Engelbert's every step. They were inside his dressing room, outside the dressing room at the stage door and in the wings just in case the enraged boyfriend intended to follow up his threat.

The increased security led to disappointment for girls hoping to sneak backstage, and the police were still out in force near Engelbert as the show rolled into Cheltenham the next night and the Worcester

(*Left*) **Gigi gets some backing from her band.** (*Aldershot News*)

(*Right*) **Aldershot News reporter Jimi Reed, right, with singer Gigi Galon in her dressing room.** (*Aldershot News*)

Gaumont on the Sunday, before a temporary reprieve with the regular Monday day off.

It was straight back into action the next day, Tuesday 31 October, with Engelbert making time to pen his weekly tour column for the *Disc and Music Echo* before hitting the road for that night's gig at the ABC Cinema in Hull.

That show went off peacefully enough, as did the trip to the ABC Lincoln the night after, but the second big hiccup was just around the corner as Engelbert suffered what he described as the moment every singer dreads, at the end of the first show at the ABC in Cambridge on Thursday 2 November. 'On stage, halfway through *The Last Waltz*, I opened my mouth and reached for the note ... but no sound came. My voice had left me.'

He struggled through the second house as best he could and retired to his digs where the doctor promptly diagnosed the dreaded flu virus and wrote him off for three nights with the grim warning that if he

Luckily enough Monday was a day off, and Engelbert needed it as he faced a non-stop seven nights, from the Gaumont at Doncaster on to the Leeds Odeon, Hanley Gaumont, Capitol Cardiff, Taunton Gaumont, Exeter Odeon and Colston Hall, Bristol, before the next day off the following Monday.

Gigi Galon made her first appearance at Exeter as Anita Harris bowed out. From San Francisco and of Filipino and Spanish descent, Galon was fresh off a stint at the Talk of the Town, but this tour did not succeed in launching her UK career. At least she had an experienced backing band, though.

The Trebletones, who had been backing Anita Harris, had been around since 1959. The UK's first glimpse of them came on a tour with Cliff when the Shadows were still known as the Drifters. Since then they had backed some big names, including Helen Shapiro, Frank Ifield, Petula Clark, Matt Munro and Bobby Rydell. The Trebletones included a fine keyboard player and musician called Ron Edgeworth who went on to marry Seeker Judith Durham. The group added three guest musicians to beef up the sound. They opened the show each night and, true to the showbiz nature of the tour, regarded themselves as an act rather than a group.

The Staggerlees, three Cornishmen who had headed north to try their luck in clubland, also fitted into the bill nicely.

Engelbert, meanwhile, travelling in his Jag, appeared to be missing the camaraderie of the bus. 'Some nights when I see everyone else piling into that coach laughing and singing and when they tell me the next day about the fun they had on the road, I get nostalgic memories and yearn to be with them,' he said. Never mind, at least there was the late night get-togethers at the hotels with Lance Percival's gags and card tricks keeping the entertainers entertained.

The dramas were behind them now as the business end of the tour settled in from the Odeon Manchester on Wednesday 15 November, on to the ABC Wigan, the ABC Chester, the Birmingham Odeon, and the Ipswich Gaumont on Sunday 19 November.

Tuesday's trip to the ABC Peterborough was followed by a two-day stint in Ireland (the ABC Belfast and the Adelphi Dublin) before the exhausted crew, without a break, headed into Hampshire for the shows at the ABC Aldershot on Friday 24 November.

There was a family atmosphere with a full house witnessing Engelbert belt out *The Last Waltz* and *Release Me* to a backdrop of non-stop screaming, with fans shelling out 10s, 12s 6d or 15s for the privilege.

The police were forced into miners-strike-type action, linking arms outside the stage door to keep back the fans when the second of the two shows was over, but by this time the tight security following the hate-mail episode had subsided enough for local reporter Jimi Reed to make it backstage for a chat with the star: Humperdinck was celebrating with a bottle of wine, pronouncing the locals 'a beautiful audience'. He even had a wry smile when Reed said that what most mid-twenties males had to say about him was unprintable. 'They all like me,' he countered, unconvincingly.

tried to sing he could lose his voice for weeks. All this in the first week of a five-week tour!

Bad news for Engelbert was good news for the Rockin' Berries who were immediately promoted to bill-toppers for the next night's show at the Guildhall in Portsmouth. The Brummie beat merchants did not let themselves down and earned some positive press (and extra work) for their sterling efforts, but tour organisers had already hired Terry Scott and Hugh Lloyd to take over at Bournemouth the next night, before Engelbert, taking liberties with his doctor's warning, grabbed his tux and set sails for his hometown of Leicester and a bonfire night gig at the De Montfort Hall.

It was a huge gamble but Engelbert was not about to disappoint fifty relatives in the audience, including his mother and father, two brothers and five of his seven sisters. A quick test of the tonsils told him his golden voice was safe and manager Gordon Mills joined him for the trek to Leicester. The voice held out, the fans loved it and there was the by now customary standing ovation for mum and dad as Engelbert took the plaudits on stage.

Engelbert Humperdinck with some sophisticated backing from his Band Of Men. (*Aldershot News*)

Engelbert Humperdinck with some of the gold records proudly hanging on the wall of his home. (Picture by David Searchfield)

with hangers-on. I remember being surprised that they were all using his real name [Gerry Dorsey], and that my daughter got his autograph.

Gigi Galon got a warm reception from the Aldershot audience and the Rockin' Berries' performance went down well. They held their own mock version of the television pop show *Juke Box Jury*, and singer Clive Lea, always at the centre of the comedy, made full use of his talent for mimicry. His impersonations of Harold Wilson and Norman Wisdom had the kids in stitches. Then the band really let themselves go with a cream pie fight on stage!

Jimi Reed wrote in the *Aldershot News*:

They put so much into their performance and are not just a group of guitarists. Off stage they are just the same – at ease with anybody and laughing at everything. The current joke was their not having a wash-hand basin in their dressing room and having to walk up and down stairs half dressed to wash their make-up off.

When I went down to see them, everything was in turmoil. The Berries were getting ready to drive back to Birmingham.

The Berries did not have far to travel the next night as the package was playing the Gaumont in Wolverhampton and then the Odeon Derby on Sunday.

The final week commenced at the Sheffield Gaumont on the Tuesday, then on to the ABC Stockton, the ABC Carlisle, the Odeon Glasgow and the Newcastle Odeon, before the finale at the Liverpool Empire on Sunday 3 December.

However, the inconveniences of life on the road, laughed off by the Rockin' Berries, had more than taken their toll on too many stars of the sixties. Before long, Jim Capaldi was to get his way. The days of the pop package show where comedians would sometimes jostle with musicians for the limelight, were indeed numbered.

Engelbert's triple scotch had wild west Cat on the rocks

This gig was typical. As at other venues, the screams reached fever pitch when Engelbert peeled off his jacket and waistcoat. One teenager rushed forward and clambered on to the stage in an effort to embrace him but was carried back to her seat where she collapsed in tears in her mother's arms.

The Aldershot audience, like the others, was 90 per cent female and several were captured in all their tearful glory by local photographer Eddie Trusler. Eddie said:

All I can remember of Engelbert's performance is just the screaming. I did go backstage to the dressing room that night and it was crowded

Engelbert Humperdinck allowed himself a quiet moment of reflection before he went on stage in the 1960s, when he would mix his favourite tipple of scotch and coke (rather heavier on the scotch than the coke) and Cat Stevens' mistake was thinking he could keep up with him. Engelbert recalls:

When the screaming starts, even some screamers have to cover their ears. (*Aldershot News*)

I was having a drink one night when Cat came in and asked what I was drinking. I told him a triple scotch and coke and he said he'd join me. I asked him if he was sure he could take it. He said yes, so I poured him one.

Unfortunately, he couldn't take it as well as he'd thought. During one of his songs he would take out a gun and spin it around like a gunslinger, but when he tried it this night his head was spinning so much that the gun went crashing to the floor several times.

Engelbert, however, noted his talent: 'Cat was brilliant. A good writer – a good artist. The fact that he screwed up with having a drink before the show was just one time. He never did it again.'

The artists had an opportunity to check each other out during the afternoon rehearsals:

We'd normally get there before any of the crowds, but there's always somebody milling, and you'd have to get through them to the stage door. It'd be normal to get there for a sound check, lighting, all that business, but in those days there weren't a good deal of sound checks. You just went on – one, two, three, four bah bah bah. It wasn't like it is today.

When somebody was doing their rehearsal you'd sit in the audience and watch them, but during their performances I'd be in the dressing room. I didn't get out for a drink – I'd bring my drinks in with me.

Cat was not the only artist to make an impression. Although their music was at opposite ends of the spectrum, Engelbert remembers being impressed with Hendrix:

I thought Jimi was an amazing musician. I loved his music and used to stand and watch him at the side of the stage. It was different for me because I'd never seen anything like that in my life and I was in awe of the kind of sounds he was producing and the way he played that guitar. He played it with his teeth and everything. I can remember him putting it behind his head and playing it, and of course after that he would burn it.

He never returned with the same guitar. It was always busted or burnt. It was a big part of the act.

So what did the crowds make of it all? 'I think everyone went well in their own way. Of course, we were all very different, but it worked.'

It is not just the passing of time that leaves but a precious few clear memories of those days for the performers, and Engelbert is not alone in stating that the pure unrelenting pace of those tours makes it inevitable that the whole thing becomes a blur:

It was very tough. There were two shows a night and there was much to do. Every night was like the night before. You'd be mobbed at the stage door. You'd have trouble getting in and out. But all of that is what

Lance Percival proves he's the all-round entertainer. (*Aldershot News*)

goes to make a successful career – having people follow you and adore you in that fashion. And it's a funny thing, to this day they're still at the stage door when I leave and I still have to struggle from the stage to get there and the security still see me to my car – forty years later!

There are people that don't want it. But to stop and sign an autograph for somebody that's been waiting a couple of hours is not a big deal, is it? I mean, if they've took the time to wait, you should take the time to sign, and I do that anyway. What other people do [who don't sign] is their misfortune, because they're missing out on giving pleasure to somebody that's been waiting for a long time.

Any backstage memories of Jimi?

We hung around a little bit, but I don't have great memories of what we did. We'd have a drink, and I used to smoke cigars back then ... and Jimi did, well, whatever he did, if you know what I mean.

Engelbert confesses that he was not close to the Walkers:

I never had a relationship with the Walker Brothers because they kept themselves to themselves and you didn't know whether Scott was going to talk to you, or not talk to you. He had a great voice, don't get me wrong, but he lacked friendliness.

The threat from the jealous boyfriend that made so many headlines and caused havoc to the security of the winter tour with the Rockin' Berries is a memory that does not survive and Engelbert laughed when reminded of it, saying:

I honestly don't remember, but then I've been threatened so many times! I wore a bullet-proof vest for three years in the States and my bodyguard wore one as well. He was a martial arts guy and we both wore one everywhere. I think I was the first British person to be given a permit to carry [a gun]. I obviously don't any more. I didn't like carrying, but they asked me to.

Engelbert recalls the stars mucking in together on the 1960s tours:

You had pokey little dressing rooms and usually you had to share it with other artists, but it was fun. Later on, when stardom became bigger, you had your own dressing room. At the beginning there was a lot of camaraderie – people sharing and caring, which doesn't happen in today's world.

I can only tell you the way it is with me. People who were playing in Vegas would come and see your show and you'd introduce them and they'd come back stage and you'd spend hours together. But today, that doesn't happen. Maybe they're working, or whatever, but when Elvis was in town he'd come and see my show and I'd go and see his show and he'd introduce me and I'd go back and have drinks with him.

Engelbert had good cause to celebrate in 1967 – the year of *Release Me* and *The Last Waltz,* his two greatest hits. Fans recall him being announced at some venues as 'the man who kept the Beatles from number one' but that was something of a double-edged sword as it earned him some hostile comments too:

That would have been the Beatles' 13th number one and along came me and stopped it. They didn't get there. They were number two. Mind you, I sold a vast amount of records. It was unbelievable. I did one Sunday Night at the London Palladium and the very next day they had orders for 80,000 [copies of *Release Me*] and the next day it was like 94,000 and the next day it would be 122,000. They don't sell them like that now. I sold two and a half million records in six weeks.

And how did the Beatles take it?

I never caught the Beatles' reaction because I didn't really know them then and I didn't really bump into them when we used to live in the same area of St George's Hill [Weybridge]. All you'd see was the dark windowed vehicles coming in and out of St George's Hill ... and I had the same thing going.

As a matter of fact, I still have the car that I used to drive at St George's Hill – EH1, my Corniche. People would drive in and out with dark windowed cars and you wouldn't know who the devil they were and the Beatles probably had several cars going in and out so they wouldn't be followed.

As the 1960s drew to a close, Engelbert outgrew the UK touring scene by the proverbial country mile. The future for him was Vegas and friendships with some of the great icons of the twentieth century – Elvis, Sinatra, Dean Martin and Sammy Davis Junior among them.

Ripened Berries saved the show

When Engelbert Humperdinck, suffering from those early tour voice problems, was unable to appear at the Portsmouth Guildhall, the Rockin' Berries found themselves in the spotlight and as frontman Clive Lea recalled, they did not let anybody down:

I remember Engelbert's voice going on that tour. Anita Harris was asked to top the bill, but she wouldn't. So we were asked to do it. We just extended our act, with more of the comedy, and it was an outstanding success. I don't think anyone asked for their money back. In fact, the story made the nationals and we ended up playing the Royal Command Performance that year, so that's an indication of how well it went.

The group's mix of comedy and music was perfect for television and they racked up eight performances on *Sunday Night at the London Palladium,* plus television specials with Des O'Connor, Jimmy Tarbuck and Forces' sweetheart Vera Lynn. So when the singles died out from 1967 they were able to find a happy home in the world of summer seasons and panto. 'They were good fun,' said Lea.

Their mix of music and comedy struck a chord with a Beatle:

When we were touring with Peter and Gordon in the mid-1960s there was a night when Paul McCartney, who was going out with Peter's sister Jane Asher at the time, came into our dressing room. He said Great act, Clive. I was made up. The last time I had seen the Beatles was in the very early 1960s when we were in Germany. We were

The Rockin' Berries before the custard pies... (*Aldershot News*)

playing the Top Ten Club in Hamburg and they were at the Star Club. We would sometimes watch each other's bands, although I can't remember talking to them much.

I remember George Harrison asking our guitarist Chuck Botfield to teach him the intro lick for *Johnny Be Goode*, which he did. I knew instantly that the Beatles were going to make it. The music was great and there was such chemistry between them.

On that 1967 Humperdinck tour were two groups who did not become household names – the Trebletones and the Staggerlees. 'They were good regular lads,' said Lea.

Lance Fortune of the Staggerlees had enjoyed some chart success as a solo performer, having a number four hit with *Be Mine* in 1960, a song that stayed in the charts for twelve weeks.

Lance Percival did more than just tell jokes: 'He'd had a hit back in 1965 – a song called *Shame And Scandal In The Family* and he would bring a guitar on stage to sing that. He was a funny man – off stage too.'

Best of all was Lea's friendship with his Rockin' Berries mates. 'We were a great team. We all got on and there would also be the social nights out. They were great.'

(*Left*) **The Rockin' Berries in perfect harmony.** (*Aldershot News*)

(*Right*) **A pie in the face for being a sleepy bulltoad... The Rockin' Berries were good mates, but they didn't mind handing out some slap with their stick!** (*Aldershot News*)

Sticking in the memory from the tour bus years are trips with Bill Haley's band the Comets and Roy Orbison's band the Candy Men, and it was the Candy Men who fell victim to one of the Berries' pranks. Lea recalled:

We were on tour and crossing the border into Scotland. We said there were haggis running wild on the moors and we had to go through an initiation ceremony – with them being Americans we were able to con them into believing that haggis were roaming the moors!

Anyway, there was plenty of snow outside and we said we had to baptise them and it involved putting snow down their trousers for luck. When we got back on the bus we gave them three choruses of *Freeze A Jolly Good Fellow*. They finally cottoned on!

Musicians crossed paths and friendships were made, but lives were too busy to keep them going: 'We would pass each other, but we were working all the time. I became friendly with Marty Wilde, but then I haven't spoken to him for twenty years.'

Lea left the band in 1970 to pursue a ten-year solo career. There was another claim to fame. He joined the Black Abbots – replacing Russ Abbot.

Let's drink a toast to each other... Gigi Galon and Engelbert enjoy a tipple. (*Aldershot News*)

Oh no you don't... Bouncer Lionel Watts, whose normal job as cinema doorman was relatively uneventful, gets to grips with a fan. (*Aldershot News*)

Nine
The Cinema Guys

Take a bow, the backroom boys

THEY WERE THE unsung heroes of the pop package tour. A small but dedicated band of workers whose task it was to ensure that the 1960s pop star looked and sounded as good as possible amidst the chaos of a High Street gig, and did not get ripped to bits by the fans.

With many of those gigs being at cinemas, all this fell to the men whose normal lot it was to check that the film spools were running properly. When the stars were appearing live on stage rather than screen and were relying on electrified instruments and creative lighting to look and sound good, a whole new set of skills were needed for these backroom boys – not least, calm and diplomacy.

Projectionists became stage and spotlight operators. The doorman, whose normal task was nothing more onerous than turfing out the odd cheeky kid who tried to trick his way in through a side door, suddenly found himself in front of the stage as the 'protection' for pop stars as 100 screaming girls tried to storm past him. Even the chief projectionist did not escape. He was often drafted in to work the curtains and liaise with tour managers and roadies to make sure everything ran smoothly. If he was lucky, that might include pointing the way to the nearest pub, for if the touring party disappeared then the staff could get to work in peace on the all-important preparations for the show. Deadlines were tight. Every second counted.

In the case of Aldershot, chief projectionist Tony Brooks directed operations from the stage, projectionist Graham Eadington-Cooke and Tony's son Colin operated the two lime spotlights (Arthur Tooke operated one on the Del Shannon show), and Fred Hobbs worked the stage lights. Bad luck, doorman Lionel Watts – you're security for the night!

To give poor Lionel at least a fighting chance, some muscle was often hired in the hours leading up to the show. Aldershot being an army town was very good news indeed. Dangled in front of an unsuspecting soldier was the prospect of some easy money – they only had to tackle some excitable girls swooning over pop stars – how difficult can that be? I wonder how many regretted it hours later when the screaming mob, dozens at a time, some armed with scissors ready to lop a coveted lock of hair, attempted to storm the stage?!

Lionel can be seen in several pictures, in his bow-tie and smart velvet-collar jacket, trying to protect the stage without hurting the girls: a tough job. Cinema staff would not have been paid extra for all this. Danger money? Forget it. There would not even have been overtime as, of course, it was all happening in their normal working hours. Did they resent it? Not a bit of it, at least if they were young and enthusiastic, as Graham Eadington-Cooke was.

Graham was twenty-four when the Hendrix show hit Aldershot, and to him it was an exciting new challenge. He laughed:

Poor old Lionel, I bet it was the hardest day's work he ever did, but I would definitely have been looking forward to it. I wasn't star struck by any means – at twenty-four, I was a little too old for that – but I liked music and it was a challenge, a live show, something different from just showing films, and Orbison and Hendrix were the two big shows.

Tony and Colin Brooks also enjoyed the challenge of those live shows. According to Tony:

We loved it because it was out of the normal run of things. It was something different. It involved extra work, but no extra money. We didn't mind that. It was exciting. To put on a stage show was a wonderful thing to us.

Tony, then aged forty-four, was not a fan of pop music, preferring instead musicals, but his son Colin – aged seventeen when the first show was staged – was in the right age bracket:

I started at the cinema in 1964 when I was sixteen, so I got to see the eighteen-only films before I should! In those days there was a chief, second, third and fourth projectionist, and I was the boy. I was quite excited when we started putting on the pop shows. I was a massive fan of the Beatles, and I liked a lot of the Mersey groups.

Colin confesses that he did not understand the music of Jimi Hendrix, but he does remember an encounter:

I was hanging about downstairs before the show and the Jimi Hendrix Experience were sitting in one of the front rows in the stalls, just talking and larking about.

They called me over and Jimi asked me to go out and get them some fish and chips. I knew Tony's fish bar was across the road, so I agreed. Jimi reached into his back pocket and pulled out a fiver – it was a lot of money then.

I didn't go out the front as it was 3 p.m. or 4 p.m. by then and there were already queues gathering. So I slipped out of a side exit and wedged the door ajar so I could let myself back in.

On my way back from the chippie I was crossing the road when about twenty girls started screaming. They seemed to be staring in my direction and then I twigged. They obviously thought I was somebody! I started running and they started running. I sprinted that 100 metres and just about made it, quickly wedging the door shut behind me.

By that time Jimi and the boys were in their dressing room. The door was open so I went in and I noticed that one of them had curlers in his hair. So that's how they got it to look like that! Anyway, I handed the food over. At least the chips must have still been hot.

The limited time to prepare for shows left the staff little chance to mix with the stars as they got ready for their soundchecks. The stars would typically arrive in the early afternoon, by which time the cinema staff would already have been briefed and hard at work. Graham said:

The bus would turn up and the unloading would begin and we'd sometimes be drafted in to help the roadies unload the equipment. After the sound-checks, the musicians would sometimes wander off in the town – probably to find a pub – but some of the bigger stars wouldn't arrive until much later in their cars.

A security guard has his arms full keeping this young girl in check. (*Aldershot News*)

Hendrix, arguably the biggest star of all, was one who arrived early on the tour bus with his mates:

As I recall it, Jimi had his trademark wide-brimmed hat and a sheepskin type coat. He certainly stood out. I was very close to him at one point, but I didn't get his autograph and I've kicked myself ever since! But you were too busy. There just wouldn't have been time.

Tony, orchestrating events from the wings, occasionally had some illustrious company:

Jimi Hendrix asked if he could stand next to me in the wings. He wanted to see one of the other acts performing. He seemed a very nice chap. He was polite and I was quite happy for him to stand there.

A major bonus meant Graham and the boys, perched on seats at the back of the stalls, were around for the soundchecks – a one-off concert for them in a way, and without the accompanying screams.

That Orbison show left another memory for Graham – the professionalism of the Big O:

Roy Orbison sounded as good on stage as he did on record, I remember that, and the atmosphere was quite lively.

Cinema manager Peter Jackson, already well into middle age, made all the right noises in the local press, welcoming the pop tours to the town. Looking back, this gave Graham quite a chuckle. He recalls a rather different Mr Jackson:

That bloke hated kids. He hated Saturday morning pictures when all the children would be in screaming their heads off. I can remember him actually turning the lights on during a film and telling them all to pipe down if it got too much. He wanted the quiet life. Get 'em in, sit 'em down, shut 'em up, get it over and chuck 'em out – that was him. He was old school. He was a typical old school manager. He even checked the fingernails of the kiosk girls!

For most of the shows, 250 seats were removed for safety reasons, reducing the 1,750 capacity to 1,500. The traditional organ at the front of the stage was covered. A loose wooden panel can be clearly seen in some of the photographs – a health and safety nightmare by today's standards.

However, despite all the chaos, the events were meticulously planned. It would all begin with a phone call from head office telling the cinema the date for the show. Then there would be more calls and visits from district managers over the next few days. Graham said:

For us, it started a couple of days before when we would be cleaning the footlights and making sure they were fully lamped up. A quick glance would tell us if a bulb had blown. New gelatines would be added to footlights and batten lights for colour. It would all be done in a morning.

Come the day, you would get in early and change all the curtains from a film show to a stage show setting. It was a fair old bit of work. They were fixed on barrels. You would have to keep hold of the ropes and I burnt my hands badly on them before one show.

We had to remove the black felt stage cloth and then sweep the stage with Dustmo – which was sawdust with linseed oil in it – to clean it. It was all very hectic. After the sound-check we would finish whatever we had to do on stage, then possibly have a sandwich, then we would be given cue sheets for the show, any additional colours for the spots and then we'd retreat to the projection room and get ready for the show.

We'd put carbon in the spotlights and then the stage manager's voice would come over the intercom, giving us instructions about the lighting and such. Then we would put the music on ready for the customers to come in.

In fact, add in the screams when the show was underway and the potential was there for everything to fall apart. ABC head office sent out speakers to every cinema so they were ready for the shows. Aldershot had eight rectangular speakers, about 4ft long, 1ft wide and 9in deep, to be fixed to the walls. They were also supplied with an amp unit, mixer, three or four microphones and stands, and three standing speakers. Then there were the bands and all their equipment. Graham recalled:

The noise was enormous. We were worried about our portholes being blown out, because they were not a fixture. They just slotted in and were held in by their own weight. But when the concerts were on, the porthole glasses would vibrate and rattle.

Stars who preferred to prepare for the shows in the peace and quiet of their humble cinema dressing room rather than head for the pub, might bring along their own record player and records to while away the hours. Unfortunately, singer P.P. Arnold, in Aldershot as a replacement for Jeff Beck on the Roy Orbison tour, left hers behind. Graham remembered:

I'm not sure who discovered them but the records were stored in the rear intake room for years, right up until the cinema closed.

There were a couple of 10in records – a Peter Sellers comedy record was one of them – and maybe twenty to twenty-five LPs, mainly jazz. You would have thought her tour manager would have followed it up, but we never got a call.

Cinema guys: Film stars... Aldershot ABC cinema colleagues, from left, Colin Brooks, Graham Eadington-Cooke and Tony Brooks. (Author's collection)

it should have been on the drummer. There was some pretty colourful language at times over that intercom!

Tony recalled:

One artist's manager went up into the projection room to personally oversee the lighting. My guess is that it was probably Engelbert's second visit.

It was all in a day's work. And it was a long day too. According to Graham:

We would have started at about 9.30 a.m. and it was probably midnight before we left. The shows may have finished around 10.20 p.m., but don't forget we had films to show the next day and we wouldn't have wanted to come in and have to change everything around again, so we did it after the show.

EMI had taken over ABC cinemas by then and they regularly sent us records, usually plugging their own artists, I'm sure. We'd play them during the intervals between films and before the pop shows. The gig nights were nerve-wracking because they were live and we wanted to get it right, but there were lots of things that could go wrong!

Rock 'n' roll being what it was, not all of the young performers stuck to the script. They might drop a song on a whim, or slot it in earlier or later if they thought it might work better. Fine for them, but a nightmare for the poor blokes up in the projection room. Graham recalled:

We'd be getting instructions by intercom from the stage on all the lighting. I would mainly work the spotlights and we followed a cue sheet. This was all very well but when the show was on they would sometimes change it without telling you and then moan because we had the wrong colour spot on, or the spotlight was on the singer when

(*Left*) **We're over here... The girls try hard to get the attention of their idols.** (*Aldershot News*)

(*Right*) **One young man has time for a smile at the camera as it kicks off all around him.** (*Aldershot News*)

Hard taskmasters they may have been, but the tour managers had a generous side:

They appreciated our efforts. Tony would often get a bottle of whisky and we'd get some beers sent up for us. They'd often give us a tip too, when it was all over – cash in hand – thanks lads!

Of course, those EMI records were a bonus too, but one potentially valuable single has long since vanished. Graham reminisced:

One of the records – it must have been about 1972 – featured a young group called Smile who were looking to make a name for themselves. Nobody had heard of them and God knows what happened to their record.

But that young band went on to be Queen and I wish I had that record now... I wonder what it's worth?

The tough guys get tough...
One girl's desperate dash
for the stage is brought to a
sudden halt by the security
team. (*Aldershot News*)

The Small Faces relax in their dressing room during the 1967 tour with Roy Orbison and Paul and Barry Ryan. (*Aldershot News*)

ASSOCIATED BRITISH CINEMAS LTD.
and/or any of its ASSOCIATED and/or
SUBSIDIARY COMPANIES

THE PROPRIETORS WILL NOT BE RESPONSIBLE
FOR ANY LOSS OF OR DAMAGE TO PROPERTY OR
FOR ANY PERSONAL INJURIES (FATAL OR OTHER-
WISE) HOWSOEVER CAUSED.

ARTISTES ARE STRONGLY ADVISED NOT TO
LEAVE VALUABLES IN DRESSING ROOMS.

Artists Interviewed

Gary Walker of the Walker Brothers enjoying a day out in London with the author in November 2006.

Wayne Fontana, pictured by the author before a gig at the Anvil, Basingstoke, in 2006.

Former Settlers singer Cindy Kent pictured by the author one afternoon in August 2005 before her Premier Radio show.

Reach out and I'll be there... The stars were almost near enough to touch on these pop nights. (*Aldershot News*)

Well, even we have to let our hair down sometimes... The St John Ambulance Brigade nurses find some time between administering first aid to hysterical love-struck teenagers for an odd spot of boogie-ing. *(Aldershot News)*

The Small Faces rocking the ABC to its rafters...
(*Aldershot News*)